HELENSBURGH HEROES

INSPIRING LIVES:
100
REMARKABLE PEOPLE
HELENSBURGH & LOMOND

Written & Compiled by
Stuart Duncan & Phil Worms

Published by Neetah Books 2017

Acknowledgements

The authors gratefully acknowledge the assistance and support of the following in the production of this book: David Stone, Emma Butterfield, Peter Ford, Garry McCormack, Geoffrey Grimmett, John Hendley, Alison Arijs, Emily Dean, Steve Niblock, Anisha Walkerley, Jan Merchant, Paul Murdoch, Clare Freestone, Peter McIntyre, Charlotte Thomas, Yasmin Atalay, Sam Maddra, Ian Rutherford, Cat Doyle, Niki Russell and the Co-op Local Community Fund and finally, Linda and Debbie for their patience, reassurance and love.

Cover design by Garry McCormack

For the many men and women whose stories have yet to be told...

Introduction

Back in 2008, when we first aired the idea of publicly celebrating the achievements of the Helensburgh & Lomond community, the responses could best be categorised as various flavours of derision, cynicism and bemusement.

Much of the criticism was aimed at the term *hero* and our choice of people for inclusion that were 'hardly household names', 'only ever *lived* in the town' and our personal favourite, which came courtesy of a journalist; 'Can you really call a town talented just because a historical figure once dropped in to buy a choc ice?'

All in all, it was pretty much to be expected. How could a mathematician be a hero? How could the life of someone who died over two hundred years ago be of relevance today?

Heroism is most often exemplified through the efforts of ordinary men and women who persistently strive to overcome whatever challenges they face, choosing not to quit, recovering from setbacks, and setting no limit on the heights they personally wish to achieve.

We've always used the term in the context of describing someone who has set an example - someone from whom we can learn and who hopefully we might one day emulate. Someone with a great story to tell.

Above all, heroes give us hope; they help define the limits of our own aspirations, they symbolise the qualities we'd like to possess and the ambitions we'd like to satisfy. Without them we might settle instead of strive, merely exist instead of truly *living*.

Every single person has the ability to become a hero - sometimes all we need is an inspiring example...and what better example than someone who may have attended the same school, walked the same streets or played for the same club as you?

If *they* can win medals for their nation, exhibit *their* art in the world's finest galleries, grace the world's greatest stages, top the music charts, build globally-renowned businesses, fight for human rights or innovate and create everything from new medicines to computer games, then why can't you?

Tales of heroes have entertained us for centuries and we hope that this book will continue in that tradition. We are proud to bring you this collection of 100 remarkable people all of whom have connections with the beautiful Helensburgh & Lomond area.

And yes - it *does* include mathematicians...

HELENSBURGH HEROES

CONTENTS

Major Phil Ashby QGM

Royal Marine Officer & Mountaineer

Born in 1970 and brought up in Helensburgh, Phil Ashby has always had a taste for adventure. Encouraged by his parents to partake in 'character building' activities – from which he often had to be rescued by older sister Penny – Phil spent much of his childhood surviving all manner of sticky situations.

After leaving Glenalmond College with excellent grades and a passion for mountaineering, Phil decided some further character building was required before starting university, so at seventeen he accepted a gap-year commission as a Second Lieutenant with the Royal Marines – making him the youngest officer in the British Armed Forces at that time. He won his Green Beret just one week after his eighteenth birthday.

Phil then accepted a Royal Marine bursary to read engineering at Pembroke College, Cambridge while continuing his officer training. Graduating top of his class, he was awarded the Commando medal for 'Leadership, Unselfishness, Cheerfulness, Determination and Courage'.

In 1995, after eleven months of arduous training, Phil was selected to join the elite Mountain and Arctic Warfare Cadre. During this period he also qualified as a Jungle Warfare instructor. He was promoted to Major at the age of 28, making him the youngest officer of that rank in the British Armed Forces.

In May 2000, during a six-month tour as an unarmed UN observer, Phil's actions brought him to international attention. After rebels had reignited the country's civil war and turned against UN representatives, Phil successfully led a daring and dramatic escape from the jungles of Sierra Leone; he was awarded the Queen's Gallantry Medal for his actions.

Upon returning to Britain he was rushed to hospital, paralysed from the waist down by a virus lodged in his spinal cord. Front-line soldiering was now impossible; his celebrated military career was suddenly at an end.

After a lengthy period of rehabilitation – during which he had to learn to walk again – Phil made a full recovery and now divides his time between successful careers as a professional mountain guide and an in-demand motivational speaker. His autobiography 'Unscathed: Escape from Sierra Leone' was a bestseller.

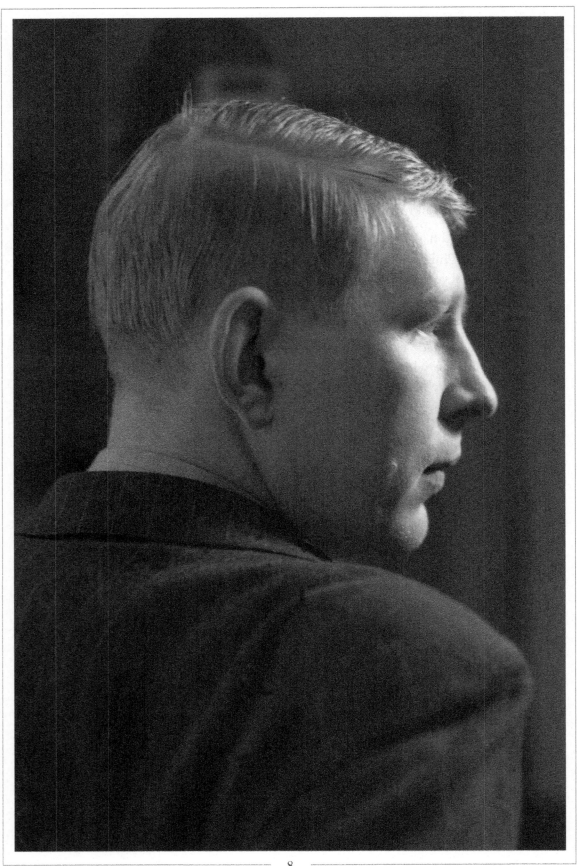

WH Auden

Poet & Writer
(1907 – 1973)

The two and half years he spent teaching in Helensburgh helped shape the career of one of the 20th Century's greatest poets.

Wystan Hugh - known more commonly as W.H. – Auden was born on February 21 1907, in York. Following his schooling in Surrey and Norfolk, he attended Christ Church, Oxford, graduating with a third class degree in English. During his time at university he joined a circle of writers that included Cecil Day-Lewis, who went on to teach at Helensburgh's Larchfield Academy.

Auden's first book, Poems, was published in 1930 with the help of T.S Eliot at Faber and Faber. Later that year, after being recommended by Day-Lewis, Auden began teaching English and French at Larchfield.

During his time in Helensburgh, Auden wrote and published his second book *Orators: An English Study*. The book is considered a classic of the period, and draws on many local people and places for its inspiration.

Auden appeared to be content with his time teaching, writing to his brother John "School mastering suits me. I am thoroughly enjoying it." One former Larchfield pupil, Norman Wright, was less enamoured with Auden as a teacher, recalling him as "rather uncouth … bit his fingernails to the quick, smoked heavily and spluttered when he spoke".

In 1939 Auden moved to the United States, where he continued to teach at a number of universities, before becoming a US citizen in 1946. His writing earned him the 1947 Pulitzer Prize for poetry and in 1956 he became Professor of Poetry at Oxford University, where his light workload – he was required to give just three lectures per year – allowed him divide the remainder of his time between the US and Europe.

He died in Vienna, Austria on September 29 1973, aged 66.

In 2008, a global search was undertaken for missing early works written by Auden whilst at Larchfield. According to two 1931 reports from the *Helensburgh and Gareloch Times*, he contributed to a school magazine he published called *The Larchfieldier*, and penned a play *Sherlock Holmes Chez Duhamel*, depicting a visit to France by the celebrated detective.

William Auld

Esperanto Poet and Translator
(1924 – 2006)

A lifelong friendship that began at Helensburgh's Hermitage Academy led to a nomination for the Nobel Prize for Literature.

William Auld, known as Bill, was born to Scottish parents in Erith, Kent on November 6 1924.

At age 9 Bill moved with his family to Glasgow, where he won a scholarship to Allan Glen's School. He was an avid reader, regularly visiting the library in Glasgow's Gorbals district, and it was there he first became fascinated with the international language Esperanto.

As a 12-year-old boy scout, Bill encountered a version of the scout promise in Esperanto, and his scoutmaster presented him with a copy of *Step by Step in Esperanto* to study.

Bill acquired sound theoretical knowledge from the book but had little chance of practical use until he moved to Helensburgh with his family in 1939.

When Bill was 16 he became friends with John Francis at Helensburgh's Hermitage Academy. John shared Bill's enthusiasm for Esperanto, and soon the two were talking exclusively in the language. The pair would eventually create The Scottish School (Skota Skolo) of Esperanto, along with poet Reto Rossetti and writer John Dinwoodie.

Fascinated with aviation, Bill joined the Youth Flying Corps in Helensburgh, leading to his voluntary enlistment in the RAF in 1942. By 1944 he was an officer flying spitfires on high-level reconnaissance missions over North Africa, teaching Esperanto to his comrades between sorties.

After the war Bill graduated with an MA in English from Glasgow University and became a teacher. In 1960 he took a post at Lornshill Academy in Alloa.

In 1952 he published his first book of poetry in Esperanto *Spiro de l'pasio* (Breath of Passion), the start of an incredible literary output of poems, anthologies, textbooks and translations. His 1956 epic poem La infana raso (The Child Race) is generally considered to be the greatest work of Esperanto literature and earned three Nobel Prize nominations in 1999, 2004 and 2006.

In 2001 Bill donated his extensive personal Esperanto collection to the National Library of Scotland.

He passed away in Dollar at the age of 81 on September 11 2006.

John Logie Baird

Television Pioneer
(1888 – 1946)

John Logie Baird was born on August 13 1888 at 121 West Argyle Street in Helensburgh.

He attended Larchfield School from the age of 11 and later enrolled in an electrical engineering course at the Glasgow and West of Scotland Technical College.

In 1916 he began work with the Clyde Valley Electrical Power Company. After failing the medical for military service, Baird left the power company to pursue various entrepreneurial interests such as his cure for cold feet - the Baird Undersock – which made him roughly £1,600, before moving to Trinidad and Tobago in 1919 where he briefly ran a jam factory.

Returning to the UK in 1920, Baird began to investigate how to transmit moving images - an idea which had first been proposed in 1878 and which had eluded inventors ever since.

By 1924, he was able to transmit a flickering image of a Maltese Cross ten feet across a room. 1925 saw transmission of the world's first true television image, the painted wooden head of a ventriloquist's dummy known as Stooky Bill.

On January 26 1926 Baird demonstrated his invention to members from Britain's Royal Institution and other visitors in Frith Street, London – the first public demonstration of a working television.

Many 'firsts' followed for Baird over the next two years - long distance transmission 1927, transatlantic transmission, transmission to a ship, mechanical colour and stereoscopic (3D) television, all 1928.

From 1929 the BBC used Baird's technology to broadcast its earliest television programming. However, his mechanical system - while undoubtedly the first form of television - had technical limitations, which in 1937 led to it being dropped by the BBC in favour of Marconi's electronic system.

Undeterred, Baird continued to innovate and was the first person to design, construct, and exhibit a multi-gun colour television tube for which a receiver was first demonstrated to the media on August 16 1944. However, despite the undoubted brilliance of Baird's colour and stereoscopic television systems, they were never implemented commercially, mainly due to the effects of World War II on the UK economy.

Baird suffered a stroke and died on June 14 1946 in Bexhill-on-Sea. He is buried alongside members of his family in Helensburgh Cemetery.

Professor Emeritus Michael Baker
TD FRSE

Academic & Author

In today's consumer-driven society, every thriving business understands that effective marketing lies at the heart of its success. Yet it is only since the early 1970s that Marketing has been valued as a professional specialism, and much of this recognition is down to one man.

Michael John Baker was born in Debden, Essex on November 5, 1935. After graduating from Durham University and completing military service, he spent six years working in the steel industry followed by four years in further education, lecturing in Marketing.

In 1968, he attended Harvard Business School in the US as a Foundation for Management Education Fellow where he was awarded the Certificate of the International Teachers Program as well as a Doctorate in Business Administration.

In 1971, Michael founded the Department of Marketing at the University of Strathclyde and was its first Head of Department, a position he held until 1988.

In 1972 Michael moved with his family to Helensburgh.

Between 1978 and 1984 he served as Dean of the School of Business Administration at Strathclyde Business School. He was appointed its Deputy Principal in 1984, Deputy Principal (Management) in 1988 and Senior Adviser to the Principal in 1991 before becoming Emeritus Professor in 1999.

Michael is a former Chairman of the Scottish Business Education Council, past Chairman of the Institute of Marketing, and Governor of the Communication Advertising and Marketing Foundation.

Winner of the Institute of Marketing's Gold Medal, Michael was also awarded an Honorary Fellowship of the Institute of Marketing in 1988 in recognition of his services and was made a Fellow of the Scottish Vocational Educational Council "In recognition of outstanding services to education in Scotland". He has also sat on the Boards of many Educational committees and organisations.

Michael is the author and editor of over 50 books and more than 150 articles and academic papers, many of which have become standard texts for students and professionals alike. He has also founded three academic journals and has acted as visiting Professor at 29 universities across the globe.

Michael continues to tour the world, lecturing and presenting marketing strategies and methodologies.

Henry Bell

Engineer & Entrepreneur
(1767 – 1830)

Any list of Scots who have helped shaped the modern world must surely include Henry Bell, whose paddle steamship PS Comet is arguably equal in significance to George Stephenson's steam locomotive Rocket.

Henry was born at Torphichen, West Lothian on 7th April 1767, into a well-known family of millwrights, builders and engineers.

During the 1780s, he served as an apprentice stonemason, millwright, ship model builder and engineer under both James Inglis in Glasgow and celebrated Scottish civil engineer John Rennie Snr in London.

Around 1790, Henry returned to Glasgow to work in building and construction in partnership with James Paterson.

In May 1806, he bought land on East Clyde Street in Helensburgh on which he built the Baths Hotel and spa, which was run by his wife Margaret until her death in 1856.

Between 1807 and 1810, Henry served as Helensburgh's first Provost during a period of positive change in the area.

In 1810 he mortgaged the hotel property for £2000 in order to fund the design and construction of a working steamship. Work on the resulting vessel, *PS Comet*, was completed the following year.

Following a successful maiden voyage in 1812 – the first commercial steamboat journey in Europe – Henry began providing regular passenger services between Glasgow, Greenock and Helensburgh, which effectively opened up the West Coast's tourist routes. Competition flourished, transforming the Clyde into the centre of steamship development and cementing its future as the world's pre-eminent shipbuilding centre.

Although his work helped shape history, Henry did not profit from it, and he often struggled financially, prompting several benefactors to raise funds on his behalf.

He died in Helensburgh on November 14 1830 at the age of 63. He was buried in Rhu churchyard following a large funeral which saw the whole of Helensburgh closed down for the day.

Evidence of this incredible life can still be found locally; there is an impressive statue over his grave, a monument sits on Helensburgh seafront, the Comet's flywheel rests on the east promenade, a street is named in his honour and his likeness is carved on the town's old Municipal buildings.

Lee Bisset

Soprano

"One of those singers who rivet one's attention from their first entrance onstage, engage the listener not only with perfect mastery of their part, but also with an accurate feel for the words and fantastic acting." Dorota Kozi ska

Soprano Lee Bisset grew up on the banks of Loch Lomond, where her parents owned and managed the Inverbeg Inn.

She developed her love for music from the age of five while attending Helensburgh's Lomond School. "My teachers gave me a solid foundation of knowledge and technique with unstinting support," she says. "They made me work hard, but it was always fun."

Having studied singing at school, Lee took a Bachelor of Music degree at the Royal Scottish Conservatoire in Glasgow as a mezzo soprano, but on graduation was advised not to continue as a singer.

Not wishing to give up on her hopes of becoming a professional artist, Lee moved to Rimini in Italy to study with baritone Romolo Castiglioni. With his help, she made the transition from light mezzo to spinto soprano, and effectively turned her voice around. A three-month stay extended to three years, which she funded by teaching English. During this period she also performed in masterclasses given by Renata Scotto, Magda Oliviero and Luciano Pavarotti.

Lee returned to the UK to complete her postgraduate studies at the Royal Northern College of Music in Manchester, where she received the Dame Eva Turner Award for Dramatic Sopranos, the Kennedy Strauss award and Webster Booth award.

In 2003 she made her professional debut singing the part of Tatyana in *Eugene Onegin* for Clonter Opera and was selected as one of twelve students to attend the internationally renowned National Opera Studio, sponsored by English National Opera.

Lee has established an international reputation for vocal stamina, versatility and for the passion, commitment and sincerity of her acting, with works by Puccini, Wagner and Janácek ät the core of her repertoire.

She has sung principal roles for, amongst others: Scottish Opera; Opera Memphis; Longborough Festival Opera; Ópera São Paulo; Opera Omaha and Opera North.

Lee lives with her family in East Sussex.

George Blake

Author & Journalist
(1893 – 1961)

An early memory of watching the ill-fated RMS Lusitania heading down the Clyde on her way to sea trials, led to a lifelong fascination with ships and the sea that both inspired and influenced George Blake's writing career.

Born in Greenock on October 28 1893, he was the fourth child of Matthew Blake and Ursula Scott McCulloch and went to school at the town's Academy.

George was studying law at Glasgow University and serving a Legal apprenticeship when the outbreak of the First World War halted his academic career. After joining the 5th Argyll and Sutherland Highlanders he was posted to Gallipoli, where he was wounded and discharged from the Army in 1917.

After the war George began a career in journalism, joining the staff of the Glasgow Evening News in 1918.

By 1922 he had published his first book, *The Vagabond Papers*, and had written three plays - *The Mother, Fledglings* and *Clyde-Built* - for the Scottish National Players. He went on to write more than twenty novels and many non-fiction works; his 1935 novel *Shipbuilders* is considered a classic, featuring in *The List's* 100 Best Scottish Books of All Time.

George and his wife Ellie moved to London in 1924 when he was appointed acting editor of the literary magazine *John O' London's Weekly*. He joined the staff at *The Strand* magazine four years later.

In 1930 George was appointed a director of Porpoise Press, a subsidiary of publisher Faber & Faber set up to encourage, publish and promote Scottish writing.

He returned to Scotland in 1932 as special features writer for the Glasgow Evening Times. The following year he began broadcasting for BBC Radio, introducing a regular feature called *The Week in Scotland*. He would later provide commentary for major events including the launch of RMS Queen Mary and the coronation of King George VI.

Between 1935 -1939, George lived at The Glenan on John Street in Helensburgh, where he concentrated on his writing career, the town providing the backdrop for his semi-autobiographical 1937 novel *Down to the Sea*.

He died aged 67 on August 29 1961.

Paddy Boyde MBE, DCM

RSM Argyll and Sutherland Highlanders
(1912 – 1986)

Regimental Sergeant Major Richard Thomas Boyde - known universally as Paddy - was born February 1 1912 in Kilcock, County Kildare. He completed his education in Scotland after his family agreed to manage a smallholding in Erskine.

In 1930 an impromptu visit to Stirling Castle saw Paddy being talked into joining the Argyll & Sutherland Highlanders by a persuasive recruiting Sergeant.

His distinguished military career would last for over 33 years and would see him receiving fourteen major military awards including the Distinguished Conduct Medal, Meritorious Service Medal, two Indian Service medals, the Africa, Italy, France and Germany Stars and two Korean Medals.

His Distinguished Conduct Medal was awarded for personal bravery during the storming of a enemy-held farm at Rosau, as the 7th Battalion of the Argyll and Sutherland Highlanders sought to capture the German village of Bienen during the Rhine Crossings in March 1945.

During the campaign Paddy led the 7th Argylls into one of their fiercest battles by starting community singing of 'Abide with Me'. One by one the men joined in until Paddy was leading a choir of more than a thousand voices.

In 1946, Paddy married his wife Cathy, eventually settling in her childhood home - Woodhead Cottage, Camis Eskan in Helensburgh.

After the end of WW2, he served in Hong Kong, Korea and British Guyana before returning to the UK in 1954.

For the next three years Paddy served as RSM at the Regimental Depot at Stirling Castle and was awarded the MBE in 1955. From 1957 until 1966, he was stationed in Europe as RSM to the British Support Unit at Supreme Headquarters Allied Powers Europe where he became a firm favourite of Field Marshal Viscount Montgomery.

Between 1960 and 1963 Paddy served in Potsdam as RSM to the British Military Mission to the Soviet Union and finally as Weapons Training Officer and Sports Officer in Rheindahlen, the headquarters of the British Army of the Rhine.

On retiring from the Army in December 1966, Paddy worked for Customs and Excise in Dumbarton.

He died in Helensburgh in 1986 at the age of 74.

Bobby Brown

International Footballer & Manager

When Scotland famously defeated the newly crowned world champions England 3-2 at Wembley in 1967 they were led by Bobby Brown, the nation's first full time manager, in charge of his first international game.

Robert 'Bobby' Brown was born March 19 1923 in Dunipace, Stirlingshire. He received his early football education at Falkirk High School under Coach Hugh Brown, an ex-league player who ran the school team along professional lines. Bobby demonstrated a real talent for goalkeeping, and signed for Queen's Park in 1939, making his league debut aged 17 against Celtic in April 1940. He established himself as the team's first-choice goalkeeper for the next two seasons, but his appearances were interrupted by the Second World War.

During the war, Bobby trained as a PE teacher at Jordanhill and qualified to pilot Fairey Swordfish planes with the Fleet Air Arm whilst playing occasional games for a Combined Services Team and as a guest player for Portsmouth, Chester, Chelsea and Plymouth Argyle.

On February 3 1945 Bobby made the first of his ten appearances for Scotland in an unofficial international against England in Birmingham. On April 13 the following year, he played what was to become the personal 'stand out' game of his illustrious career when 139,468 spectators watched Scotland beat England 1–0 at Hampden Park in what was dubbed the *Victory International*. His first official cap was against Belgium in January 1946, the last amateur player to win one.

At the end of the 1945–46 season Bobby left Queen's Park for Rangers FC, where he played for ten years, winning eight major honours including Scottish football's first domestic treble in 1948-49, under the legendary manager Bill Struth. He ended his playing career with Falkirk in 1956.

1958 saw Bobby begin a successful eight-year period as Manager of St Johnstone which led to his appointment as Scotland Manager from 1967 until 1971.

When his football career ended Bobby became a successful businessman, opening a coffee shop – *WhichCraft* - in Helensburgh, where he has lived since 1970.

Bobby has been inducted into both the Scottish Football and the Rangers FC Halls of Fame.

Jack Buchanan

Entertainer

Rumoured during the 1930s to be the world's highest-paid entertainer, Walter John 'Jack' Buchanan was born in Helensburgh on April 2 1890, to parents Walter and Patricia.

His West Argyle Street home was only a short distance from that of his lifelong friend John Logie Baird. The pair attended the town's Larchfield School together before Jack moved to Glasgow, his mother having been forced to sell the Helensburgh home to settle her late husband's gambling debts.

On leaving school, Jack joined the same firm of auctioneers where his father had worked. However he soon realised that his future lay elsewhere, and he began channelling his energies into productions with the Glasgow Amateur Operatic Society.

In 1911 he made his first professional appearance at Glasgow's Panopticon, then a notoriously tough music hall. Even though this debut did not go well, an undeterred Jack moved with his family to London in order to better learn his craft.

Rejected for military service because of poor health, Jack spent the war years touring and appearing in theatre productions including *Tonight's the Night, Bubbly* and *Tails Up*.

In 1925 he became involved in the pioneering work being undertaken by John Logie Baird, investing heavily in his old friend's company Television Limited, which he continued to support even after Baird's death.

Over the next three decades, Jack dominated the British entertainment industry. He acted, produced and directed on stage and film, conquered both the West End and Broadway, built and managed theatres and helped develop the UK film industry.

On August 31 1957 Jack returned to Scotland to perform *I Belong to Glasgow* as part of Scottish Television's launch night. This was to be his final public performance; he died in London just seven weeks later. His ashes were scattered from the deck of the Queen Mary in recognition of the more than 50 transatlantic crossings he had made during his career.

Jack is perhaps best remembered for his role in MGM's classic 1953 musical *The Band Wagon*, joining Fred Astaire on screen as the top British and American song and dance men of their day.

Rachel Buchanan MBE

Disability Rights Campaigner
(1915 – 2008)

Having a learning disability in Britain was considered a real stigma well into the 1950s. Over the years this situation has improved, largely because a small group of people have tirelessly and selflessly campaigned to ensure that men and women with learning disabilities have the same rights, choices and opportunities as others.

Rachel McInnes was born at Kilmahew Cottage, Cardross on September 20 1915 to parents Donald and Margaret.

Following her education at Cardross Primary School and Hermitage School in Helensburgh, Rachel embarked on a nursing career, training at Glasgow's Belvidere and Western Infirmary Hospitals before going on to study midwifery in Perth.

In 1944, she joined the Queen Alexandra's Military Nursing Service India. She served in Asia and was one of the first allied nurses to enter a Japanese prisoner of war camp in Singapore.

Like many people who had experienced first-hand the horrors of the POW camps, Rachel rarely spoke of it, opting to recall that her time in Asia was spent attending many dances and chasing doctors. Whilst in Singapore, Rachel witnessed one of WW2's defining moments – the surrender of the Japanese Generals to Lord Mountbatten on September 12, 1945.

In 1950, Rachel married optician William Buchanan and had four children: Mairi, Douglas, Donny and Robert. It was the birth of Donny in 1956 that was to have the most profound effect on the couple's lives.

Rachel and William joined the Dumbarton branch of Scottish Association of Parents of Handicapped Children, which later evolved into ENABLE. Realising that more needed to be done at a local community level, the couple became founding members of a Helensburgh & District branch in 1960.

In addition to her local work, Rachel championed national causes such as daytime provision for children with significant needs, shared holidays and community housing, as well as actively supporting projects such as the establishment of Stewart Home in Cove – Scotland's first respite home for children and adults with learning disabilities.

Her pioneering contribution to ENABLE Scotland was recognised with an MBE in 1986.

Rachel Buchanan passed away in Helensburgh on May 25 2008 aged 92.

David Caldwell

Artist

"I paint primarily from life. This direct engagement with the sitter is an important part of my work. A portrait is not only about achieving a likeness but also about capturing the sitter's individual energetic presence."

Artist David Caldwell was born in Helensburgh on the January 27 1977. Encouraged by his school art teacher, he went on to study at the prestigious Glasgow School of Art between 1994 and 1998 and at The Princes' Drawing School – now the Royal Drawing School – between 2003 and 2005, where he obtained an MA level diploma.

"As a child I was always drawing" He says. "If it was raining outside I would be content knowing that I could while away the hours lost in drawing. Through observing other people's reactions to my work I realised that I clearly had a talent. Henceforth I always felt that it was my duty to nurture and share this talent. I have always been grateful that I have this clear direction in my life; that I enjoy what I do and that I feel like I am doing exactly what I am supposed to be doing."

David has built a reputation both nationally and internationally through his work within the genres of landscape and figuration, citing the work of Corot, Constable and Cezanne as influences. He is also renowned for his self-portraits, which he completes periodically, mapping his development both personally and artistically.

He has exhibited extensively throughout the UK and overseas, with his work appearing regularly in shows at the National Portrait Gallery, The Mall Galleries and The Royal Glasgow Institute of The Fine Arts.

David has been the recipient of several major residencies and awards, including the prestigious Royal Society of Portrait Painters' Bulldog Bursary, The Founder's Purchase Prize 2010 and the Regional Award 2014 at the ING Discerning Eye.

In addition, his work has been shortlisted for The BP Portrait Award, The Threadneedle Prize, The Lynn Painter Stainers Prize, The Seven Investments Management Award, The W. Gordon Smith Award and the Ruth Borchard Self Portrait Prize.

David currently lives and works in London.

Professor Horatio Scott Carslaw
ScD DSc LLD

Mathematician & Academic
(1870 – 1954)

Science students attending lectures at the University of Sydney do so in the Carslaw Building - named in the 1960s after an inspirational and visionary Helensburgh-born mathematician and educationalist.

Horatio Scott Carslaw was born February 12 1870 at the Free Church Manse in Helensburgh to the Rev. William Henderson Carslaw and wife Elizabeth.

A bright pupil, Horatio entered Glasgow University from Glasgow Academy in 1887, having been placed sixth in the General Entrance Bursary competition. He graduated in 1891 with a first class honours degree in Mathematics and Natural Philosophy, having also won the Cunninghame Gold Medal in pure mathematics in 1890 as well as the Eglington Fellowship.

Horatio enrolled at Emmanuel College Cambridge to study mathematics, before returning to Glasgow University to teach in 1896. In 1897 he spent a year studying in Rome, Palermo and Göttingen where he was introduced to techniques in Theoretical Physics that would influence his later research. He was elected a Fellow of Emmanuel College in 1899.

In 1903, aged 33, Horatio left Scotland for Australia having been appointed Chair of Pure and Applied Mathematics at the University of Sydney, a position he was to hold until his retirement in 1935.

On his arrival, Horatio found he'd inherited a run-down department and set about transforming it. During his tenure, the University's Faculty of Science grew in size and reputation, with Horatio also helping to develop the NSW Secondary Education system. He received honorary doctorates of Science from Adelaide in 1926 and of Laws from Glasgow University in 1928.

1905 saw the publication of the first of his ten books, whilst his most important work - the impressively-titled *Introduction to the Theory of Fourier's Series and Integrals and the Mathematical Theory of the Conduction of Heat* - followed a year later.

Horatio married in February 1907 but his wife Ethel sadly died within five months of the marriage.

The effect on Horatio was profound and after a three-year hiatus, he resumed his research, publishing many papers on both mathematics and education until his death at his home at Burradoo on November 11 1954 aged 84.

Jean Clyde

Actress
(1889 – 1962)

On Friday November 6, 1936 at 3.35 pm, the BBC – using John Logie Baird's television system – broadcast scenes from the Royalty Theatre London's production of *Marigold*. It was the first drama officially televised by the BBC, and it starred an actress who spent much of her life living in Helensburgh.

Jean Clyde was born in Glasgow on March 17 1889 to Scottish theatre producer/actor John Clyde and his wife Mary. Jean was one of six children, two of whom, David and Andy, would also find fame in the entertainment business.

Jean first appeared on stage aged six months when she was carried on during her father's production of the play *Jeannie Deans*. She began her acting career at the age of five, travelling around Scotland with her Father's theatre company.

At 19 Jean joined another touring company, this time playing the role of Scottish heroine Bunty Biggar in the play *Bunty Pulls the Strings*. It was a role with which she would become synonymous, with more than a thousand performances in London and across the UK, Africa and Australasia.

Jean married her co-star David Urquhart and the couple, together with fellow actor Abie Barker, formed a new theatre company, The Bunty Comedy Company, which toured extensively for two years.

Between 1918, when she made her American stage debut, and the early summer of 1927 when she decided to retire, Jean performed at theatres across the globe, specialising in strong Scottish female lead parts, including many of JM Barrie's heroines.

Jean was however soon lured from retirement to take the lead role of *Mrs Pringle* in the play *Marigold*. A huge west end hit, Jean would go on to play the role throughout the UK, the US and Canada. *Marigold* caught the attention of BBC programme planner Cecil Madden, who was seeking 'a play from London' for the corporation's opening week of programmes from Alexandra Palace.

Jean married her second husband Edward McQuaid in 1934. She returned to Helensburgh after his death in 1949, and lived in the town until she passed away on June 24 1962 at the age of 73.

Andy Clyde

Actor
(1892 – 1967)

Impeccable comic timing, versatility and stamina provided Andy Clyde with a forty-year Hollywood career, stretching from the age of silent movies to the giant television networks of the 1960s.

Andrew Allan Clyde was born in Perthshire on March 25 1892, but grew up in Helensburgh in a theatrical family. His father John ran a successful touring company in which Andy performed with siblings Jean and David.

Andy first visited America in 1912 as part of a touring company in the play *The Concealed Bed*. He returned in 1920 at the invitation of his close friend James Finlayson - a former member of his father's company - to join Mack Sennett's roster of comedians, where he eventually became the studio's most popular comic.

By his early thirties, Andy had developed his 'Pop' persona - an elderly character with a drooping moustache, grey wig and spectacles - so successfully that he would continue to play him in various forms throughout his long career.

On September 23 1932, Andy married Elsie Tarron, with whom he'd worked on the Sennett comedies *The Lion's Whiskers* and *A Taxi Scandal*. The couple bought a mansion, nicknamed Clyde Manor, and would later have a son, John Allan Clyde, who sadly died aged just nine years old.

Between 1924 until 1956 Andy starred in more two-reel short comedies than any other actor, first with Mack Sennett, then with Educational Pictures and from 1934 with Columbia Pictures.

In the 1940s, Andy gravitated toward outdoor and western adventures and is well remembered for his roles as a comic sidekick, whether teamed with William Boyd as California Carlson in the *Hopalong Cassidy* series or with Whip Wilson in Monogram Pictures' series of westerns.

After the last of his 225-plus films was released in 1956, Andy embarked on a television career, starring in series as diverse as *Lassie*, *The Real McCoys* and *No Time for Sergeants*.

He passed away in California on May 18 1967 at the age of 75, seven years after he had been inducted into the Hollywood Walk of Fame. His star can be found at 6758 Hollywood Boulevard.

Stephen Conroy

Artist

Stephen Conroy is one of the most prominent artists to emerge from the contemporary Scottish figurative art movement of the mid-1980s.

Noted for the depiction of solitary human figures in formal poses, his work is steeped in tension, poignancy and mystery; intense images featuring simple stark backgrounds, bold geometric patterns and a central single figure. His influences include Francis Bacon and fellow 20th Century Scottish artist James Cowie.

Born at Braeholm, Helensburgh in 1964, Stephen attended St Patrick's High School in Dumbarton before enrolling at the Glasgow School of Art in 1982, where he was to achieve both public and critical acclaim before finishing his post graduate studies in 1987.

Stephen came to wider prominence in 1985 when the *New Image Glasgow* show brought together the works of six Glasgow School of Art artists: Stephen Barclay; Steven Campbell; Ken Currie; Peter Howson; Adrian Wiszniewski and Stephen himself. Collectively this group became known as *The New Glasgow Boys,* establishing a bold new figurative style in Scottish art.

In 1986 his work won first prize at the Royal Academy's British Institute Fund Awards and his subsequent degree show sold out. In 1987 he was the youngest artist to be included in the Scottish National Gallery of Modern Art's *The Vigorous Imagination New Scottish Art* exhibition. A year later, Stephen's work was included in the British Council's *New British Painting* exhibition, which toured major US venues between 1988 and 1990.

Stephen's first solo exhibition was held at London's prestigious Marlborough Fine Art gallery in 1989, and he has exhibited worldwide ever since. In 1998 he was awarded the Prince Rainier III Grand Prize for International Contemporary Art by the Prince Pierre of Monaco Foundation.

His work is both highly regarded and sought after, and can be found within major public collections such as The Metropolitan Museum of Art in New York, the National Portrait Gallery, the Whitworth Gallery and the Fleming Collection.

Stephen returned to Helensburgh in 1989, purchasing a property in Prince Albert Terrace, where more than half the works for his second London exhibition were painted. He now lives in Cardross.

James Copeland

Actor & Writer
(1918 – 2002)

James Gordon Copeland was born in Grant Street, Helensburgh on May 1 1918.

James, known as Jimmy, left Helensburgh's Hermitage school to help his Grandfather, a shoe repairer, before working in the Blackburn Aircraft Factory in Dumbarton during the Second World War. He had stints as a policeman and a water bailiff whilst pursuing his passion for acting in amateur dramatic productions with the Scottish People's Theatre in Dumbarton.

He enrolled to study drama at the Glasgow College of Dramatic Arts and began his career at the Glasgow Citizens' Theatre in 1951. He made his professional film debut playing a fisherman in the 1953 production Laxdale Hall, a romantic comedy starring Ronald Squire.

A forty year acting career in films and television followed, with Jimmy coming to prominence as The Mate in 1954's BAFTA nominated classic Ealing production *The Maggie,* one of several films he made between 1953 and 1991, the last being acclaimed US film *Rage in Harlem* starring Forest Whitaker, Robin Givens and Gregory Hines.

Between the late 1950s and 1970s Jimmy was a familiar face on UK television, appearing in many classic shows including *The Flying Doctor, Dixon of Dock Green, Softly Softly, Z Cars, The Brothers, Doctor Who, Doctor Finlay's Case Book* and *Take the High Road.*

Jimmy was made a Freeman of the City of London in 1955 and also became Grampian TV's start-up presenter and continuity announcer in 1961.

In addition to his acting accomplishments, Jimmy was a talented writer, penning songs and scripts and adapting plays. Although he shied away from the term 'poet', he was an expert on the works of Robert Burns, William McGonagall and Robert Service and published two books of verse, Some Work in 1972 and James Copeland's *Shoogly Table Book of Verse* in 1983.

Jimmy married Helen in 1941 and the couple had two children. Son James, who adopted his mother's middle name Cosmo as his stage name, is a successful actor who also owned and ran a health food store in Helensburgh.

Jimmy died peacefully after a long illness in Twickenham on April 17 2002 aged 83.

AJ Cronin

Author & Physician
(1896 – 1981)

A childhood defined by religious turmoil and experience as a doctor helped a Cardross man become one of Britain's most successful novelists.

Archibald Joseph Cronin was born July 19 1896 at Rosebank Cottage in Cardross, the only child of a protestant mother and catholic father. The family moved to Prince Albert Terrace in Helensburgh where they lived until Archibald was seven, when his father passed away.

Having attended Dumbarton Academy, Archibald won a Carnegie Foundation Scholarship to study medicine at the University of Glasgow, where he met his future wife, physician Dr Agnes Mary Gibson. He graduated in 1919, having served as a probationary surgeon in the Naval Reserve during the war.

Archibald took up his first position in Tredegar, a mining town in South Wales and in 1924 was appointed Medical Inspector of Mines for Great Britain. Between 1926 and 1930 he practised in London, until poor heath led him back to Scotland to convalesce. During this period he wrote his first novel, 1931's *Hatter's Castle,* which was an instant commercial success and enabled him to become a full-time author.

His subsequent novels - many optioned by Hollywood - sold millions worldwide, making him a very wealthy man. Much of his work was autobiographical in nature.

His most famous novel, 1937's *The Citadel,* drew on his experiences of the inequalities in healthcare between Tredegar and Harley Street and was the biggest selling book of the 1930s. It is often cited as one of the inspirations for Britain's National Health Service, whose main architect Aneurin Bevan – coincidentally perhaps – had served on the Board of the Hospital where Archibald had worked.

In the late 1930s he moved to the USA , taking out citizenship before moving to Switzerland in the 1950s, where he continued to write until his death on January 6 1981.

Despite his substantial wealth, Archibald never forgot his roots and remained a lifelong supporter of Dumbarton FC.

He found fresh fame in the 1960s when the BBC drama *Dr Finlay's Casebook -* based on his novella *Country Doctor* - became one of the longest-running series on British television.

Cecil Day-Lewis

Poet and Author
(1904 – 1972)

Make our hearts as bright and brave,
As the mountain and the wave,
So Scotland may be proud of you.

It may not rate as his most memorable work, but these three lines from the Larchfield Academy school song were written in 1928 by the then newly appointed teacher – and future Poet Laureate - Cecil Day-Lewis.

After accepting the £300 per year teaching position at the school, Cecil settled with his wife Mary into their first marital home, 128 West King Street in Helensburgh, a town he described as the 'Wimbledon of the North'.

He was born on April 27 1904 in Ballintubbert, Ireland, the only child of the Rev. Frank. C. and Kathleen Day Lewis. Cecil moved with the family to England in 1906 and was educated at Sherborne School and Wadham College, Oxford.

On leaving Oxford in 1927 he taught at various schools - including his stint at Larchfield - until 1935, when he began to concentrate full-time on writing, editing, and political activism. Despite his brilliance as a poet, his financial independence was achieved through writing detective stories. In 1935, he published the first of twenty bestselling crime novels under the pseudonym Nicholas Blake, most of which featured detective Nigel Strangeways - a character whose traits resembled those of Cecil's great friend WH Auden.

In his youth Cecil adopted communist views, becoming a member of the Communist party from 1935 to 1938, and his early poetry reflected his preoccupation with social themes. During the war he worked as an editor for the Ministry of Information, despite having being placed under MI5 surveillance for his earlier political associations.

In the post-war years, Cecil received great academic and official recognition. He delivered the Clark Lectures at Trinity College, Cambridge, was appointed Professor of Poetry at Oxford 1951 and in 1964 was the Charles Eliot Norton Professor of Poetry at Harvard.

In 1968 he was appointed Poet Laureate, a position he held until his death on May 22 1972.

Day-Lewis's two marriages produced five children, including Academy Award-winning actor Daniel Day-Lewis, food writer Tamasin Day-Lewis, and television critic Sean Day-Lewis.

Charlotte Dobson

Yachtswoman

Charlotte Isobel Dobson was born in Rhu on June 5 1986 and educated at Helensburgh's Lomond School, where she enjoyed sport, particularly tennis, and was selected for the Scottish junior squad. Charlotte began to focus on sailing after watching the Scottish Nationals at Helensburgh Sailing Club.

Sailing with - and competing against – her near neighbour and fellow club mate Luke Patience helped hone Charlotte's skills and she was selected for the Scotland national squad at the age of 14.

In 2001, she won a bronze medal in the Laser Radial class at the Youth World Championships before winning silver medals in the same competition in both 2002 and 2004. By 2005 she was ranked seventh in the ISAF world rankings and in 2007 she finished tenth in the ISAF World Championships in Portugal.

Charlotte was shortlisted for Team GB for the 2008 Beijing Summer Olympics, narrowly missing out on selection. Despite some good results over the next four years, including silver at the 2010 World Cup, Charlotte once again missed out on selection for the London 2012 games in the individual Laser Radial class after finishing behind Alison Young in the Olympic regatta at Hyeres.

After completing her Psychology degree at Edinburgh University, Charlotte switched from the Laser to compete in the 49erFX class with Sophie Ainsworth. The pair won bronze in the 2013 World Cup in Mallorca.

In March 2016, Charlotte and Sophie were selected as Britain's first ever representatives in the new 49erFX women's event in the Rio de Janeiro Olympic Games, where they finished eighth. Speaking about her time at the Rio games, Charlotte said "I really believe it has been a magical experience, from start to finish, way more than I expected it to be".

In January 2017, Charlotte teamed up with Saskia Tidey, who had previously sailed for Ireland at the Rio games - in a bid to qualify for the 2020 Tokyo Olympics.

In a little over 6 months since they first sailed together the pair had won 49erFX bronze in the Sailing World Cup, gold in Kiel and silver at the European Championships.

Fionna Duncan

Jazz Musician

Described as 'One of the greatest jazz singers Scotland has ever produced', and 'The Fairy Godmother of Scottish Jazz', a singer from Garelochhead has been at the heart of Britain's Jazz scene ever since the Swinging Sixties.

Fionna Duncan was born during a blackout at the Temperance Hotel, Garelochhead, in November 1939. After spending her primary school years on the Gareloch, the family moved to Glasgow, where Fionna attended Rutherglen Academy. Whilst at school she appeared as lead in several Gilbert and Sullivan operas and became heavily involved in the *Ballad and Blues Club,* citing Louis Armstrong, Carmen McRae and Tony Bennett as early influences.

After leaving school, Fionna sang with various jazz bands before becoming the resident vocalist with the Lindsay MacDonald Modern Jazz Quartet in 1955. In 1956, during a business trip to United States, Fionna performed on network TV and was subsequently offered a contract with Riverside Records, which she turned down.

Returning to Scotland in 1957, Fionna performed on the weekly BBC Glasgow live programme Skiffle Club with The Joe Gordon Folk Four. After a short time singing with Glasgow's Steadfast Jazz Band, she joined The Forrie Cairns All Stars and later The Clyde Valley Stompers.

During the 60s and early 70s, Fionna was host at London's famous Georgian Club, singing with the giants of the jazz scene at the time – Humphrey Lyttelton, Kenny Ball, Warren Vache, Grover Washington, Sweets Edison and many others. She also sang regularly with The Georgian Dixielanders, who were supported by the Beatles when the band played in Liverpool.

A decade later, and back in Glasgow, Fionna became a full time vocalist, recording, touring at home and overseas before forming her own trio in 1985.

Keen to encourage the next generation of jazz singers, Fionna has been running workshops for aspiring vocalists since 1996; her work recognised by a Parliamentary award for services to Jazz Education in 2008.

Fionna returned to the family home in Garelochhead in 1993 and continues to perform in the style that led to her being crowned Best Jazz Vocalist at the 2009 Scottish Jazz Awards.

Kirsten Easdale

Singer & Musician

"A voice to die for…pure enunciation, clarity of tone and the ability to squeeze the last drop out of every note – sheer undiluted magic…" is how *Celtic World* Magazine describes Rosneath musician Kirsten Easdale.

Kirsten Jane Dickson was born on the June 4 1966 in Glasgow, growing up in Uddingston, where she played the violin and sang in both school and church productions.

After leaving school, Kirsten performed in several amateur choral productions before turning professional in 1991. During the early 1990s Kirsten was a member of folk group Whisky Fingers and Dundee-based band The Cutting Edge before becoming a founder member of the highly-regarded Celtic band Calasaig in 1997.

Calasaig recorded several critically acclaimed albums in some of the world's finest facilities - including Sun Studios in Memphis - and performed at major venues and festivals across the globe.

Renowned for her beautiful and powerful voice, Kirsten appears on many albums, including her own solo recording *Be Not Afraid,* a celebration of Celtic Christian music.

Kirsten was lead vocalist on four of the twelve volumes of Linn Records' *The Complete Songs of Robert Burns*, a landmark project to record every song written or edited by Scotland's National poet. Kirsten has performed for The Centre for Robert Burns Studies at the University of Glasgow and has toured with Dr Fred Freeman's live production of *The Complete Songs.*

Between 2005 and 2008, Kirsten put her career on hold to care full time for her son Stuart, who has Autism; however she still found time to help out with local music projects as and when she could.

Since 2009, Kirsten has been performing and recording music and poetry alongside accordionist Gregor Lowrey and vocalist Rod Paterson as a founder member of Bring In The Spirit. The band, which was formed in Helensburgh, takes its name from the *Before and After Dinner Grace,* which Robert Burns composed for the Landlord of The Globe Inn in exchange for his own dinner.

When not performing with Bring in The Spirit, Kirsten works with the charity Music In Hospitals, bringing live music to patients throughout Scotland.

Major
George de Cardonnel Elmsall Findlay VC

Soldier & Public Servant
(1889 – 1967)

George de Cardonnel Elmsall Findlay was born on August 20 1889 at Boturich Castle, Alexandria, the third son of Major Robert Elmsall Findlay and Jane Cecilia Louise Scott Findlay.

He was educated at St Ninian's Preparatory School at Moffat and Harrow School – where he won two shooting competitions in 1907 and 1908 – and at the Royal Military Academy, Woolwich, where he won the revolver shooting competitions in 1908 and 1909.

George was commissioned into the Royal Engineers on January 30 1910, serving in the 5th Field Troop as Assistant Adjutant for Musketry at Chatham. He was awarded the Military Cross for gallantry at the Battle of Passchendaele in November 1917 and further awarded a Bar to the Military Cross in October 1918 for offensive work culminating in the taking of the Hindenburg Line.

On November 4 1918, during the final offensive of the war, George was awarded the Victoria Cross for conspicuous bravery and devotion to duty when, under intense enemy fire and despite being wounded, he placed a bridge across the strategic Sambre-Oise canal, enabling the allied forces to continue with the northern attack.

He retired from the Army in 1939 before serving again at the start of World War II. After retiring yet again in 1941 George once more returned to active service in 1943.

After the war, George dedicated much of his life to the Helensburgh community, having moved to Drumfork House in Colgrain in the 1930s.

For 23 years from 1941, George represented Cardross and Craigendoran ward as a councillor, and was appointed a Deputy Lieutenant of Dunbartonshire County in 1957. He supported many local charitable organisations, most notably the British Legion, where he served as President of the Helensburgh branch for a number of years before being appointed Life President.

In 1959, George married Constance Clark, just eight years before his death on June 26 1967 aged 77 at Drumfork. He is buried in the family plot in Kilmaronock Churchyard, Gartocharn.

George's Victoria Cross, Military Cross (with bar) and other medals are on display at the Royal Engineers Museum in Chatham, Kent.

Malcolm Finlayson

Footballer
(1930 – 2014)

Malcolm Finlayson was born on June 14 1930 in Alexandria. Malcolm loved football and played for his school and the local boys brigade teams. By the time he was 11 he was playing in Under 17 teams.

Despite being a talented pupil, Malcolm's parents could not afford to keep him at school and he was sent to work in the Shipyards at 14. He continued playing football and at 15 he had trials with both Dumbarton FC and Celtic FC Reserves.

Whilst playing for Renfrew Juniors he was invited to London for a trial with Millwall FC by a watching scout. Malcolm signed a contract in February 1948 and made his first team debut against West Bromwich Albion on February 28 aged just 17. He would go on to make over 250 appearances for the club, a figure that would probably have been higher had it not been for his period of National Service.

In August 1956, when Wolves, managed by the legendary Stan Cullis, sought an understudy for their England keeper Bert Williams, they beat several first division rivals to sign the then 26 year old Malcolm for £3,000.

Limited to 13 first team appearances in the 1956/57 season at Molineux, he played the entire 1957/58 season as first choice keeper, winning the English First Division title. He would play over 200 games for Wolves, winning another league title in 1958-59 and the FA Cup in 1960, before retiring in May 1964.

Rather than socialise with team mates after training, Malcolm spent his afternoons studying business – a decision which helped him make his fortune as a very successful businessman post-football.

Malcolm died in Dudley in the West Midlands on November 26 2014 aged 84, two years after his wife of thirty five years, Iris, had passed away aged 82. The couple had kept a family home in Rhu for more than 20 years.

In 2013, Malcolm was inducted into the Wolves Hall of Fame. As a player he was renowned for his bravery, distribution and shot stopping and was described as 'the greatest keeper never to play for Scotland'.

Sir James George Frazer

Social Anthropologist
(1854 – 1941)

James George Frazer was born in Blythswood Square, Glasgow on January 1 1854 to parents Daniel and Katherine.

In the mid-1860s his father purchased Glenlea at 16 East Argyle Street in Helensburgh. James loved his new home and spent many hours after school roaming the nearby countryside.

James was first educated at Springfield Academy and then enrolled at Larchfield Academy in Helensburgh. There he was tutored by headmaster Alexander Mackenzie, excelling in Latin and Greek.

In 1869 he entered Glasgow University and studied Latin under George Gilbert Ramsey, Rhetoric under John Veitch and Physics under Lord Kelvin before graduating in 1874.

In 1874 James moved to Cambridge and began studying at Trinity College. He graduated with first-class honours in 1878, and was elected to a Fellowship the following year.

He then moved to London to study Law, mostly in an effort to please his father. He was called to the Bar in 1882, but never practised.

In 1890 James published what would become his most celebrated work *The Golden Bough*, a wide-ranging, comparative study of mythology and religion.

James spent the next six years traveling extensively in Europe before returning to Cambridge, where he met and married Elisabeth Johanna de Boys on April 22 1896.

In 1904 James studied Hebrew under the tutelage of Robert H. Kennett, and in 1908 he was elected to the Chair of Social Anthropology at the University of Liverpool. James, however, never liked the city, and he returned to Cambridge a year later.

In 1914 James received a Knighthood, and spent the war years in a small flat in Middle Temple, a courtesy of his nominal membership of the Bar. After the war, the couple travelled throughout Europe pursuing his research. Then in 1930 while giving a speech at the annual dinner of the Royal Literary Fund, James was suddenly struck blind. His eyesight never fully returned.

Despite this handicap, James engaged others to write his dictation and continued on with his work. He maintained his unstinting output until his death on May 7 1941 at Fen Causeway in Cambridge.

Tom Gallacher

Playwright & Writer
(1934 – 2001)

"When I first left Scotland in the 1950s, the establishment here didn't want Scottish plays unless they were about Mary Queen of Scots." – Tom Gallacher

Tom Gallacher was born in Alexandria on February 16 1934, the family moving to Garelochhead when he was a year old.

After his schooling, Tom trained as a draughtsman and worked at Denny's Shipyard in Dumbarton, but, influenced by his mother's love of language and the spoken word, he soon decided on a complete career change and began working as a journalist – beginning with a job at the local *Helensburgh Advertiser* newspaper.

During this period Tom discovered he had a talent for writing plays, a skill that solidified during his time as an actor, writer and producer at the Dumbarton People's Theatre.

His love of the theatre and his passion for words led him to becoming a full time playwright and director for the stage, television and radio. His first significant success being the production of his play *Our Kindness to Five Persons* at the Citizens' Theatre, Glasgow, in March 1969.

Tom had a splendid disregard for the ordinary and his characters were always sharp, articulate, arrogant and full of ideas. He was very keen to inspire people through what he called the 'access of spirit', giving his audience the sense of the possibilities of life.

Plays such as *Revival, Mr Joyce is Leaving Paris, Schellenbrack* and *The Only Street,* brought Tom international renown, and he spent much of his time working in Denmark, Germany, Canada and London before returning permanently to Garelochhead in 1975, where he was to live until his death in October 27 2001 at the age of 69.

In his later years, Tom turned his attention to prose, publishing a collection of short stories in the mid 1980s.

Theatre would, however, always remain his first love and Tom, fiercely proud of his roots, was a passionate exponent of the Scottish Arts Scene, once stating that "the burgeoning riches of oil off the Scottish coast accomplished a sea change in the Arts as well . . . Scottishness was an asset, not a liability".

Major John Gilmour DSO MC and two bars

Royal Air Force Pilot (1896 – 1928)

John Gilmour was born June 28 1896 at High Mayfield, 23 East Montrose Street, Helensburgh, the son of tobacco merchant John James Gilmour and Isabella Inglis.

Having spent his early childhood in Helensburgh, John attended the distinguished Loretto School in Musselburgh in August 1910, where he displayed a keen athleticism, representing the school in both the Rugby XV and Fives and obtaining the rank of Sergeant in the Officer Training Corps.

In December 1914 John left Loretto to join the Argyll and Sutherland Highlanders regiment with the rank of second lieutenant. One year later on December 21 1915, he transferred to the Royal Flying Corps and was assigned to 27 Squadron, the sole unit equipped with the Martinsyde G100 or 'Elephant' as it was more commonly known.

Despite its size and ungainly nature, John scored three victories in the G100 in September 1916, receiving the Military Cross on May 26 1917 for his prowess as a bombing formation leader. He would later receive a further two bars for bravery and devotion to duty during the conflict.

Late in 1917, John was assigned to 65 Squadron RAF as a flight commander and after a fourteen-month gap since his last victory, downed two enemy craft in his Sopwith Camel on December 18 that year.

By June 29 1918 John had claimed 31 victories, which quickly became 36 with an incredible 5 victories in a forty five minute period on July 1 1918, earning him the Distinguished Service Order.

John was promoted to Major and was transferred to 3 Flight School, effectively signalling the end of his active service. On July 30 1919 John had a brief tenure as an air attaché in Rome before his last formal posting with No. 216 Squadron RAF in the Middle East.

Little is known of John's life following this posting and before his tragic death by his own hand some nine years later.

Major John Gilmour died of cyanide poisoning at 26 St James Street, London on February 24 1928 aged 31. His death certificate described him as of being of independent means but unsound mind.

Norah Neilson Gray

Artist
(1882 – 1931)

Inspired as a child by the beautiful flowers in her Helensburgh garden and by the stories of fairies and Celtic spirits told to her by her Nanny, Norah Neilson Gray grew up to become an internationally renowned artist.

Described as Scotland's 'foremost woman painter', Norah was considered a leading member of the group of female designers and artists – including Margaret and Frances MacDonald, Jessie M. King, Jessie Wylie Newbery and Bessie MacNicol – now widely known as the 'Glasgow Girls'.

Born on the June 16 1882 at Carisbrook in West King Street, Helensburgh, Norah began her studies under the guidance of two local art teachers – Miss Park and Miss Ross – at 'The Studio' in Craigendoran.

In 1901, Norah enrolled in the life class at the Glasgow School of Art, where she studied until 1906 when she joined the staff, teaching fashion design and drawing.

By 1910 she had a studio in Bath Street, Glasgow, holding her first solo show at Warneuke's Gallery in the city. In 1914 she became a member of the Royal Scottish Society of Painters in Watercolour.

The horrors of the First World War compelled Norah to produce some of her finest and most powerful work. During the war she served as a volunteer nurse in France with the Scottish Women's Hospitals organisation. One of her most celebrated works from this period, *Hôpital Auxilaire* 1918, is on permanent display in Helensburgh Library.

Upon returning to Glasgow in 1921 she became the first woman to be appointed to the hanging committee of the Royal Glasgow Institute of the Fine Arts. This period was to prove extremely fruitful for Norah; she won the Bronze medal for her portrait The Belgian Refugee in 1921, followed by a Silver medal for *La Jeune Fille* at the 1923 Paris salon, a feat that no other female artist had achieved.

Sadly, Norah's life was cut short at the height of her powers when she died from cancer aged just 48 on May 27 1931. She had continued painting at the family home on Loch Long right up until her untimely death.

Laura Grieve

Digital Supervisor

Laura Grieve was born in Glasgow on August 5 1969, and spent 16 formative years of her life in Helensburgh. She was a pupil at Hermitage Academy, where she shared a class with future film maker Tom Vaughan.

After leaving the Academy, Laura continued her education at Oxford Brookes University, where she studied Fine Art & Anthropology, and spent time at both the University of the Aegean and the University of Northern Colorado.

After graduation, Laura joined Sony Computer Entertainment Studio Liverpool, the oldest and second-largest development house within SCE's European division. The studio is best known for the WipeOut series of futuristic racing games, for which Laura helped develop the 3D Graphics.

In 1997 Laura left Liverpool and moved to San Francisco, where with six friends she co-founded a video game company called Shaba Games. From humble beginnings on Shotwell Street in San Francisco, Shaba Games weathered storms and celebrated triumphs to become one of the world's most innovative games producers. Its members have worked on such critically acclaimed, best-selling titles as *Tony Hawk Pro Skater 3, Wakeboarding Unleashed* and *Spider Man: Web of Shadows.* The company was eventually sold to the Activision in 2002, where it survived as a standalone games studio until its closure in October 2009.

After leaving the games industry Laura was invited to add her considerable creative skills to an animated feature being developed by DreamWorks studio. The film was about an unlikely hero in the shape of a big green ogre – *Shrek.*

Shrek was an instant and huge success right from its release in 2001 and it helped establish DreamWorks as a major player in the field of film animation, particularly computer animation. It was the first film to win an Academy Award for Best Animated Feature.

Since the release of the original *Shrek*, Laura has worked on all of its sequels as well as the *Madagascar* series, *Megamind* and *Mr Peabody and Sherman.*

Laura is currently a Digital Supervisor for DreamWorks, and in her own words is enjoying 'working with an amazingly talented and incredibly lovely bunch of geeks and artists'.

Sir James Guthrie FRSA

Artist
(1859 – 1930)

James Guthrie was born on June 10 1859 in Greenock, the youngest child of the Rev. John Guthrie and his wife, Ann. Unlike many of his artistic contemporaries he did not study in Paris and was instead mostly self-taught, although he was mentored for a time by James Drummond in Glasgow and John Pettie in London.

James was elected as an artist member of Glasgow Art Club on 1 November 1880, elected Vice President in 1886, President in 1897, and an Honorary Member on 25 April 1904.

By 1883 he was a central figure of a group of artists that was to become known as The Glasgow Boys. The group caused a sensation with their first group exhibition with their bold use of colour and naturalistic technique.

James was elected associate of the Royal Scottish Academy in 1888, and a full member in 1892. In 1902 he succeeded Sir George Reid as RSA president, and used his influence to bring about improvements in the facilities at the National Galleries of Scotland. He was knighted the following year.

In 1885 James turned his attention to portraiture, and attempted to capture the character of his sitters rather than displaying a superficial technical virtuosity. At this time he also began working in pastels, at which he became greatly accomplished. Several of the pastels Guthrie produced during this period feature the everyday lives of the middle classes who lived around Helensburgh.

Many of James' most important works have connections with the town. *A Highland Funeral, To Pastures New, In the Orchard* and *Midsummer* were either painted in a studio on East Clyde Street or feature friends who lived in the town.

James married Helen Newton Whitelaw in 1897, and the couple had one son. In 1898 James was part of the committee that eventually grew into the International Society of Sculptors, Painters and Gravers, of which James McNeill Whistler, a great influence on James, was President.

Following the death of Helen's mother in 1906, the couple spent every summer living in her family home, Rowmore in Rhu, where James passed away aged 70 on September 6 1930.

Herbert Guthrie-Smith

Naturalist & Farmer
(1861 – 1940)

William Herbert Guthrie-Smith was born in Helensburgh on March 13 1861, the eldest child of John Guthrie Smith, a wealthy insurance broker, and Anne Penelope Campbell Dennistoun.

After private tutoring and time at an English preparatory school, he attended Rugby School, where he showed early interest in the natural world.

In 1880 Herbert and schoolmate Arthur Cuningham sailed together for New Zealand.

In September 1882 they paid £9,750 for the lease of Tutira, a rundown bracken-covered sheep station of 20,000 acres in central Hawke's Bay. The station was hardly viable at first, and Cuningham soon quit, and Herbert took on Thomas Stuart as his partner. Over time they slowly improved Tutira's pastures and flocks, and were able to acquire the leases of two neighbouring properties in the late 1890s, increasing the size of the station to about 60,000 acres.

In 1901 Herbert made a trip back to Scotland, and on October 1 married a distant cousin, Georgina Meta Dennistoun Brown. In 1903 He took sole control of Tutira, which was by then a profitable enterprise with 32,000 sheep. His brother Harry joined the station, allowing Herbert to turn his energies to natural history. He concentrated on Tutira and its abundant bird life, studying and photographing a wide range of native species and their wild habitats to produce a comprehensive book collating 40 years' collected records and observations to give a complete account of Tutira station. *Tutira: The Story of a New Zealand Sheep Station* was published in 1921.

The book was acclaimed both within New Zealand and internationally, winning recognition as a provocative and unique work. Tutira's story was considered typical of the changes wrought by European settlement of New Zealand.

During his life Herbert and his family made several journeys to Britain and Europe. While travelling back to New Zealand from one such trip in 1927, Herbert's wife died in a shipboard epidemic and was buried at sea.

Herbert died at Tutira on July 4 1940.

The 2,000 acres that remained of Tutira station were left in trust to the New Zealand public as an educational and recreation reserve.

John Hammersley

Mathematician
(1920 – 2004)

John Michael Hammersley was born at Dee Bank in Helensburgh on March 21 1920 to parents Guy and Marguerite. The family moved to Bishop's Stortford about five years later.

He was sent to Sedbergh boarding school in 1934, where his interest in science and mathematics led to the award of a scholarship to Emmanuel College, Cambridge. His studies were interrupted by the start of World War II, and he was called up in 1940.

In 1941 John was commissioned into the Royal Artillery. Posted to an anti-aircraft gun site near Worsham, he applied himself to the use of wireless and radar in gunnery, and introduced several improvements on current practice in gunnery calculations that greatly increased accuracy. He left service with the rank of Major.

In 1948, John was appointed to Trinity College where he remained a Fellow until his death. It was over a Sunday lunch in Oxford that he met Gwen Bakewell, who became his wife in 1951.

John became Principal Scientific Officer at the Atomic Energy Research Establishment at Harwell in 1955 before returning to Oxford in 1959 as a Senior Research Officer in the Institute of Economics and Statistics. He received many honours, including election to the Royal Society in 1976.

John was a pioneering mathematician of enormous intellectual power. He was passionately involved in creating mathematics to solve practical problems. Despite his love of rigorous analysis, he did not hesitate to turn when necessary to using calculators, and he was a master of both the mechanical desk calculator and the early computer, once claiming for himself a world record for keeping a computer at Bell Labs in the US working without breakdown for 39 hours.

During his career he held visiting positions at Princeton University, the University of Illinois, Bell Laboratories and the University of California. He was awarded an ScD by Cambridge University in 1959, the von Neumann medal for applied mathematics by the University of Brussels in 1966, the gold medal of the Institute of Mathematics and its Applications in 1984, and the Pólya prize of the London Mathematical Society in 1997.

John died aged 84 on May 2 2004 at the John Radcliffe Hospital in Oxford.

Sir Joseph Dalton Hooker
OM GCSI CB PRS

Botanist & Explorer
(1817 – 1911)

Sir Joseph Dalton Hooker was born June 30 1817 in Halesworth, Suffolk, the second son of Sir William Jackson Hooker and Maria Turner.

Joseph moved to West Bath Street in Glasgow when his father William was appointed Regius Professor of Botany at Glasgow University in 1820. During the summer months between 1831 and 1836, the family lived at Burnside on Campbell Street in Helensburgh.

A passion for botany was kindled when Joseph began attending his father's lectures aged just seven. He was educated at Glasgow High School, studied medicine at Glasgow University and graduated in 1839. His first position was as Assistant Surgeon aboard HMS Erebus for Captain James Clark Ross's Antarctic expedition.

Upon his return he was invited by Charles Darwin to classify the plants Darwin had collected on his expeditions. It was to be the start of a lifelong friendship, Joseph later publicly defending and supporting Darwin's *On the Origin of Species.*

Over the next 60 years Joseph came to be regarded as one of greatest scientists of the age.

In 1855, he was appointed Assistant Director of The Royal Botanic Gardens in Kew, later serving as Director between 1865 and 1885. He became President of the Royal Society in 1872, received a Knighthood in 1877 and in 1907 he received the Order of Merit.

Sir Joseph died in Berkshire on December 10 1911, and is buried next to his father at Kew Green.

He never forgot his time spent in Helensburgh and remained lifelong friends with Sabina Smith, who had lived at the Baths, and whose father kept a yacht, the *Amethyst*, on the Clyde. In a letter to Sabina dated February 4 1899, Sir Joseph, then aged 81, wrote: "Do you remember our blackbird hunts in the hills above Helensburgh? Our games in the conservatory in the Baths where Bell's steam engine lay? The Amethyst? The dogs Copper and Combie? I should indeed like to visit you in Helensburgh."

He was to return two years later, recalling:" The quondam village has grown into a town, but the neighbourhood is little changed, and is as beautiful as before."

Sir William Jackson Hooker
KH FRS FRSE FLS

Botanist
(1785 – 1865)

William Jackson Hooker was born in Norwich on July 6 1785 to parents Joseph and Lydia.

He was educated at Norwich Grammar School, and developed an interest in natural history whilst learning estate management in his native Norfolk. On his 21st birthday he inherited an estate of his own, and this afforded him the opportunity to indulge his interests.

William's first botanical expedition was in the summer of 1809, when he travelled to Iceland. Unfortunately all his collected samples, drawings and notes were destroyed by a fire on the voyage home. Further expeditions to Italy, France and Switzerland in 1814 were to prove more successful.

William married Maria Turner in 1815, and the couple set up home in Halesworth in Sussex, where William set about developing a herbarium. In 1816 he published *British Jungermanniae*, the first of his many scientific works.

In 1820 William accepted the chair of Regius Professor of Botany at Glasgow University, a position he held until 1841. According to his son – the equally prominent botanist Sir Joseph Dalton Hooker – William lectured only between May and July each year; spending the rest of his time on his writing and research and with family and friends – usually in Helensburgh.

A keen and strong walker, it was not unknown for Sir William to set out on Sunday and walk the 22 miles from the town to Glasgow to ensure he would be present for his 8 am Monday lecture.

During his time at the University, William was instrumental in the development of Glasgow's Botanic Gardens which saw its collection increase from 3,000 to 12,000 species.

In 1836 he was knighted for his services to both Glasgow University and to botanical science.

In 1842 William left Scotland when he was appointed the first official Director of the Royal Botanic Gardens at Kew. During his time as Director, the size of the Gardens increased from 10 to 75 acres with new glasshouses, a large arboretum and a museum of economic botany added to the site.

Sir William died in London at the age of 80 on August 12 1865.

Gareth Hoskins OBE

Architect
(1967 – 2016)

It is entirely appropriate that Helensburgh, rich in the architecture of Mackintosh, Paterson and Leiper, should also have been home to one of the most influential British architects of the early 21st Century.

Gareth Hoskins was born in Edinburgh on April 15 1967, where he spent his formative years. He left school to train as an architect at both the Glasgow School of Art and the University of Florence.

In 1992 he joined Penoyre and Prasad as an associate, and after spending six years with the company in London, he returned to Scotland and set up Gareth Hoskins Architects in Glasgow. It was not long before Gareth's talent was publicly recognised, winning UK Young Architect of the Year in 2000.

In 2003, five years after establishing his practice, Gareth and his family moved to Helensburgh.

Through a series of major competition wins Gareth Hoskins Architects became one of the UK's leading design practices, delivering projects as varied as the Mackintosh Interpretation Centre at The Lighthouse, Robin House at Balloch, Culloden Battlefield Memorial Centre, the Athletes' Village for the Glasgow 2014 Commonwealth Games and the multi award winning National Museum of Scotland redevelopment.

2008 was to be a particularly memorable year for Gareth. He had the honour of representing Scotland at the Venice Biennale with his critically acclaimed 'Gathering Space', won UK Architect of the Year, topped Architecture Scotland's Power 100 list and became the first Architect to collect the Arts prize at the Glenfiddich Spirit of Scotland Awards.

In 2009, Gareth was appointed as an Academician of the Royal Scottish Academy, and in 2010 was awarded an OBE in the New Year's Honours List.

Gareth passed away suddenly at the age of just 48 on January 9 2016 in Edinburgh Royal Infirmary.

As both architect and resident, Gareth was always willing to contribute to local projects. Prior to his death, he had been working closely with a Helensburgh community group Friends of Hermitage Park on a £3M project to restore the only urban park in Argyll & Bute to its former splendour.

James Howden Hume

Businessman & Yachtsman
(1903 – 1981)

James Howden Hume – known to his friends as Jimmy - was born in Glasgow on March 30 1903 son of James and Agnes.

Given the full name of his father, James was also named in part after his uncle, the illustrious inventor and engineer, who founded James Howden & Co. Ltd. in 1854. The Glasgow Company remains a leading manufacturer of heat exchangers, industrial fans and rotary screw compressors, with factories and offices in 17 countries.

James Howden Hume Jr., as he was then known, was appointed Managing Director at the age of 31 in 1934, a post he held for the next 30 years before becoming Chairman of the Board when his older brother Crawford retired.

Jimmy and his wife Katie came to live in Helensburgh after buying Cromalt in East Clyde Street from the executors of Neil Munro's estate in 1930. It was to be their family home for the next 42 years.

A flair for financial management that, combined with Crawford's gifts for engineering and James Sr.'s business acumen, saw Jimmy steer the company through the difficult depression of the 1930s. It was during those darkest economic times that a wage crisis at the company was narrowly averted when a new contract came through for Howden to supply the boilers for the new Battersea power station in London.

In addition to his business skills, Jimmy was also an enthusiastic and gifted Olympic yachtsman who was instrumental in the introduction of the Dragon class yacht to the Clyde. Whilst on a business visit to Sweden in the early 1930s, Jimmy discovered that many of the yachtsmen there were racing in an exciting new type of vessel that was designed by Johan Anker.

On his return to Glasgow, Jimmy and fellow businessman Bill Paisley persuaded several other yachtsmen to purchase Dragons, and Jimmy sailed the first one to be imported, called Anita. It wasn't long before McGruer's Yard in Clynder began building these three-man, fast keelboats. In 1948, it became an Olympic class and the boats still being enthusiastically sailed world-wide.

Jimmy died aged 78 on May 28 1981.

Colin Hunter ARA RSW

Artist
(1841 – 1904)

With the Firth of Clyde as his inspiration, Colin Hunter's ability to capture the melancholy mood of the sea on canvas led him to become one of the most accomplished seascape and marine painters of the Victorian era.

Colin was born in Glasgow on July 16 1841, the youngest of five children. In 1844, owing to failing health, Colin's father moved the family to Clyde Street in Helensburgh, where he opened a library and bookshop and became the town's Postmaster.

Captivated by his environment, Colin devoted all of his leisure time to drawing the sea lochs and mountains that surrounded him. After leaving school, he spent four years in a Glasgow shipping office before departing at the age of twenty to pursue his dream of becoming a full time artist.

Virtually self-taught, Colin befriended J. Milne Donald, then one of the West Coast's most famous artists, who encouraged him at every opportunity.

Colin's work, featuring many local Helensburgh scenes, was by now attracting the attention of the Royal Academy, where he exhibited his first painting in 1868. Later that same year he established a studio in Edinburgh.

He returned to Glasgow in 1873 for his marriage to Isabella Young, at which famed architect and Helensburgh resident William Leiper acted as witness. The couple went on to have four children, one of whom, John Hunter Young, also became a renowned artist.

By the late 1870s, Colin had become extremely successful, with several galleries competing to purchase his works, and in 1877 he commissioned the building of a large house and studio in London's fashionable Kensington. After becoming a member of the Royal Watercolour Society in 1882, he was elected Associate Member of the Royal Academy in 1884, where he would exhibit every year until his death, showing nearly 100 paintings.

His most famous works included *Trawlers Waiting for Darkness* (1873), *Their Only Harvest* (1879) and *Signs of Herring* (1899).

In later life Colin suffered a stroke, which paralysed his right hand. He died aged 63 on September 24 1904 at Lugar Lodge, Melbury Road in Kensington and was buried in Helensburgh.

Kenny Hyslop

Musician

Adopting 1950s-style baseball shirts and covering a song written by the team behind many Bay City Rollers hits, led a Scottish band, featuring a Helensburgh musician, to the top of the UK charts.

Kenneth John Hyslop was born on February 14 1951 in Helensburgh.

Kenny began playing the drums at the age of twelve, citing legends John Bonham of Led Zeppelin, Keith Moon of The Who and Clyde Stubblefield - best known for his work with James Brown - as his main inspirations.

In 1972 he joined the Glasgow band Salvation with Midge Ure; in 1974 the band changed its name to Slik. After a failed debut single, and a change of image, the band signed for Bell records. Their first single for Bell Forever and Ever topped the UK charts in February 1976. An intense marketing campaign followed and Slik became overnight teen sensations, being voted New Band of the Year by readers of the Sun.

Slik split in 1977, with Kenny leaving to play with both the Zones and the Skids before joining Simple Minds for the first part of their *Sons And Fascination* 1981 tour.

Before he left the group, he recorded a song with Simple Minds that he himself had inspired. Kenny used to record late night radio music shows on cassette, which were then played on the band's tour bus. One particular show featured a funk track with an unusually catchy brass riff which became the basis of Simple Minds' hit *Promised You a Miracle*, which the band recorded in January 1982.

Following his departure from Simple Minds later that year, Kenny formed a new band, Set The Tone and later played with One O'clock Gang.

Disillusioned with the UK music industry, Kenny left for Canada with blues band Big George and The Business, returning to the UK in 1999.

For the next eighteen years Kenny ran a very successful drum school at Glasgow's Carlton Studios before leaving Scotland for the Philippines in 2017.

Kenny was very supportive of Helensburgh Heroes and its objectives, and in 2009 he produced the community-led recording of David Bowie's iconic song *Heroes* for the Charity.

Hazel Irvine

Broadcaster

In 2007 this former Hermitage Academy pupil was described by the Royal Television Society, on receiving its prestigious Sports Presenter of the Year award as, 'The consummate all-rounder. Whichever sports she is covering, she demonstrates enthusiasm and exemplary professionalism. She knows her sport, she puts in the homework and she is a formidable asset to the BBC.'

Hazel Irvine was born on May 26 1965 in St Andrews. She moved to Cardross with her family when she was young and was educated in Helensburgh before graduating with an MA Honours degree in Art History from the University of St Andrews.

Hazel's broadcasting career began in 1986 as a production assistant with Radio Clyde. She moved into sport a year later when she joined Scottish Television as a reporter.

An integral part of television sports coverage of all major sporting events since the 1990s, Hazel has covered 14 Winter and Summer Olympics, Commonwealth Games, FIFA World Cup finals, UEFA European Championship finals and the London Marathon.

Hazel is now one of BBC Sport's most experienced, versatile and recognisable broadcasters and the face of its snooker and athletics coverage. She was also a mainstay of the BBC golf team and lead anchor of the sport between 2009 and 2017.

Hazel's many other credits include *Grandstand, Sunday Grandstand, Final Score, Football Focus, Wimbledon* and *Ski Sunday*.

In addition to her role at BBC Sport, Hazel hosted coverage of the 60th anniversary of the D-Day landings in 2004, and has presented three magazine programmes – BBC2's *The Air Show,* health and wellbeing series *Feeling Good* and *Outside Now.* She has hosted BBC Scotland's *Children In Need* programming and anchored the channel's Millennium Night coverage.

Much in demand for corporate work, Hazel has acted as MC at the Royal Television Society's Sports Awards, the industry's most prestigious evening. She received the RTS Award for Best Regional Presenter/Reporter in 1999 and was named Sports Presenter of the Year at the RTS Sports Awards of 2006.

Hazel has representative honours in golf, netball and athletics and gained a full vest for athletics from Scottish Universities.

James Jardine

Medal of Honor Recipient
(1837 – 1922)

For many historians, the Confederate Army's surrender of Vicksburg, Mississippi on July 4 1863 marked a turning point in the American Civil War. One man who participated with distinction in this historic event was 26-year-old James Jardine from Helensburgh.

James was born in Sinclair Street in Helensburgh on April 16 1837, the eldest son of Graham Jardine, a sawyer, and his wife Mary.

In the early 1850s, the family left Helensburgh and moved to America, where James was to spend the rest of his life.

After enlisting in the Union Army at Toledo, Ohio, on September 5 1861, James saw action in many battles in the Western Theatre and Atlanta campaigns of the Civil War, suffering serious injuries on three separate occasions.

But it was his actions during the siege of Vicksburg on May 22 1863 that led to him receiving America's most prestigious military decoration, the Medal of Honor.

General Grant, Commander of the Union Armies, ordered an assault on a Confederate encampment at Vicksburg. The plan called for a storming party of volunteers to build a bridge across a ditch and to plant ladders against the enemy embankment in advance of the main attack.

One hundred and fifty men – including James – volunteered. More than half were killed by heavy Confederate fire, the remainder left trapped for several hours in the ditch they had been sent in to bridge.

First Lieutenant James Jardine was awarded his medal for 'Gallantry in the charge of the volunteer storming party'.

Recalling the incident in a later interview, he said: "I got a bayonet prick in the knee which I have felt to this day. That was the only thing worth speaking of, though they drew blood on me in five different places and there were nine bullets that passed through my clothes without striking my body."

After leaving the Army, James travelled to Colorado to mine for silver and went on to work in a Toledo winery until the early 1900s.

He died at the age of 85 on December 9 1922 and is buried at the Ohio Veterans Home Cemetery in Sandusky.

Deborah Kerr

Actress
(1921 – 2007)

Deborah Jane Kerr-Trimmer was born in Glasgow on September 30 1921 to Captain Arthur Trimmer and his wife Kathleen Rose. The family lived for three years with Trimmer's parents at Nithsdale on West King Street in Helensburgh.

A shy child, she found an outlet in acting and at 15 she enrolled in the Hicks-Smale Drama School, taking lessons in acting, ballet and singing. After focusing on acting she was soon appearing in Shakespearian plays at the Open Air Theatre in Regents Park.

At one such performance Deborah attracted the attention of director Robert Atkins and talent scout John Gliddon, who offered her a five-year film contract, which she signed on November 1 1939. She was immediately cast in Michael Powell's film *Contraband* but her part was eventually cut from the film. Her first screen appearance was as Jenny Hill in the 1941 adaptation of George Bernard Shaw's *Major Barbara*.

She soon became a British cinema star, with roles in *The Life and Death of Colonel Blimp* in 1943 and *Black Narcissus* in 1947. It was during this period that Deborah met Squadron Leader Anthony Bartley, the couple marrying in November of 1945. They divorced in 1959, with Deborah marrying author Peter Viertel in 1960.

In 1947 she made her Hollywood debut in *The Hucksters*, followed by *Edward, My Son* in 1949 and *Quo Vadis* two years later. Deborah soon tired of playing 'English Rose' types, and made the most of her adulteress role opposite Burt Lancaster in 1953's *From Here to Eternity*. In 1956 she played one of her best-remembered screen roles as Anna in *The King and I*.

More success followed in such films as *Heaven Knows, Mr. Allison*, *An Affair to Remember* and *Night of the Iguana*. She retired from mainstream movies in 1968.

After some stage and TV work in the 1970s and 1980s, Deborah's final film role was in 1986's *The Assam Garden*, after which she retired from acting altogether.

After a record six Academy Award nominations without a win, Deborah was finally awarded an Honorary Oscar in 1994, and became a CBE in the 1997/8 New Years Honours List.

She died in Suffolk aged 86 on October 16 2007.

Andrew Bonar Law

Prime Minister
(1858 – 1923)

Born in the colony of New Brunswick and resident of Helensburgh, Andrew Bonar Law remains to date the only British Prime Minister to have been born outside of the British Isles.

Andrew Bonar Law was born September 16 1858 in Rexton, New Brunswick to the Reverend James Law and his wife Eliza.

At the age of 12, Andrew left Canada to live in Helensburgh with his late mother's cousins – the Kidstons, who were wealthy merchant bankers in Glasgow. The family helped find Andrew a job with a Glasgow iron merchant and loaned him the money to buy a partnership. An interest in politics led Andrew to join the Glasgow Parliamentary Debating Association.

In 1888 he moved out of the Kidston household and set up his own home at Seabank on East Clyde Street in Helensburgh.

In 1891, at the age of 33, Andrew married Annie Pitcairn Robley at Helensburgh's West Free Church. The couple set up home in Seabank but on the death of Annie's father they bought his house, Kintillo, in Suffolk Street in Helensburgh.

Bonar Law's interest in politics had increased during the 1890s, and after inheriting a large sum from one of the Kidston brothers he was able to consider running for Parliament. In 1900 he was elected Conservative MP for Glasgow Blackfriars and was made Parliamentary Secretary to the Board of Trade in 1902.

He lost his seat in the 1906 General Election, but returned to represent Dulwich following a by-election later in the year. Though hit hard by the death of his wife in 1909, he continued his political career and won the Conservative party leadership in 1911.

At the outbreak of World War 1 he offered the government the support of the Conservatives in a coalition and was given senior positions in David Lloyd George's new war cabinet.

The coalition was re-elected by a landslide following the Armistice, but Conservative withdrawal in 1922 forced Lloyd George to resign and Andrew became Prime Minister. He lasted just 209 days in office, resigning due to ill health in May 1923.

Andrew died on 30 October 30 1923. As a former Prime Minister, his ashes were interred in the Nave of Westminster Abbey.

William Leiper

Architect
(1839 – 1916)

William Leiper was born in Glasgow on 21 May 1839. He was educated by his father and at Glasgow High School and served his architectural apprenticeship with Boucher & Cousland in Bath Street Glasgow. In 1859 he moved to London, working for John Loughborough Pearson and William White for approximately one year each.

William's reputation was immediately established in 1864 when he won a competition to design Glasgow's Dowanhill church. The church is now Cottiers Theatre, named after famous glass and interior designer Daniel Cottier who had worked with William.

A series of churches and mansions followed, all more or less influenced by the Gothic revival. Examples of his churches can be seen at Whiteinch, Camphill, Lanark, and Brechin. William went on to design Partick Burgh Hall and several further mansions, including the impressive Cairndhu and Dalmore in Helensburgh.

In 1880, he was chosen to design interiors for Czar Alexander's yacht Livadia, which was built at John Elder's shipyard in Govan. More commissions were to follow – both for churches and private homes - before William took a break from architecture around 1870 to focus on art, producing and exhibiting numerous works in watercolour and oils.

He was lured back into architecture in the late 1880s to design Templeton's carpet factory on Glasgow Green, an exotic mixture of red brick, terracotta, and coloured Mosaic based on the Doge's Palace in Venice. In November 1889, shortly after completion, a freak gust of wind brought the building's main facade down onto nearby weaving sheds, killing 29 people.

During this period, William also designed a block of offices for the Sun Insurance Company at the corner of Renfield Street and West George Street; his design winning a silver medal at the Paris International Exhibition of 1900.

William was elected Fellow of the Royal Institute of British Architects in 1881, Associate of the Royal Scottish Academy ten years later, and Royal Scottish Academician in 1896.

William never married. After a protracted illness that stemmed from serious blood poisoning in 1903, he was forced to retire completely in 1909.

He died at his home Terpersie, Helensburgh on May 27 1916.

Robin Lloyd Jones

Writer & Teacher

"Astonishing imaginative brilliance." was how the Times described this long time Helensburgh resident's first novel.

Robin Lloyd Jones was born in London on October 5 1934, and spent six years of his early childhood in pre-independence India whilst his father served as an Indian Army officer.

In 1946 Robin returned to Britain and completed his education at Blundell's School, Tiverton, Devon and at Cambridge University, where he graduated with an MA in Social Anthropology.

Robin moved to Scotland in the early 1960s and studied for a diploma in Education at Jordanhill College. He became a teacher of History, Geography and Modern Studies, and for several years he also taught Creative Writing at Glasgow University.

Robin moved to Helensburgh in 1965 and taught at Hermitage Academy between 1966 and 1970, when he was appointed Director of Dunbartonshire's Curriculum Development Centre, the first of its kind in Scotland.

He published his first novel *Lord of the Dance* in 1982. The novel was critically acclaimed, winning both the BBC Bookshelf Award for First Novel and a submission for the Booker - now Man Booker - Prize.

As an author, Robin's body of published works includes fiction, non-fiction, short stories and radio drama. His novels lean towards the historical genre rather than the contemporary, and feature three recurring themes: the wisdom of having doubts and of not being certain you are right; the relationship between illusion and reality and trickster figures.

His non-fiction writings focus on both the environment and the wilderness, reflecting his love of the mountains, wildlife and the sea. Robin is both an accomplished mountaineer and a qualified sea-kayaking instructor.

In addition to his successful teaching and writing career, Robin is a passionate supporter of free speech. From 1997 to 2000 he served as President of the Scottish branch of PEN International, a worldwide organisation promoting literature and defending freedom of expression. Robin was also president of the Scottish Association of Writers between 1981 and 1986 and chaired the Scottish Centre's Writers in Prison Committee for 17 years before finally retiring in 2009.

Jimmy Logan OBE

Entertainer
(1928 – 2001)

Jimmy Logan OBE was born James Short in Glasgow on April 4 1928. His parents were a music hall act - Short and Dalziel - and his Aunt, from whom he took his stage surname, was Broadway star Ella Logan.

At seven years old he was selling programmes for his father's summer show in Northern Ireland, and by the age of twelve he was appearing in a wartime charity show with Sir Harry Lauder, the legendary Scot who became his idol.

A comic, dancer and singer, Jimmy soon established himself in the forefront of Scottish show business, notching up a record number of performances of the famed *Five Past Eight* shows that were staged each summer at Glasgow's Alhambra Theatre,

On television, he starred in ITV's *Saturday Showtime* in 1956, and from 1957 to 1961 in the BBC's *Jimmy Logan Show* - much of it written by Jimmy himself.

He also starred in more than 150 radio shows with fellow comic and close friend Stanley Baxter.

In 1964, Jimmy purchased Glasgow's Empress theatre for £80,000. He refurbished it at great personal cost, opening it as the New Metropole. Further development was blocked by planning authorities and the spiralling costs almost ruined him.

His first acting role was alongside Gordon Jackson in the film *Floodtide* in 1949. He featured in 1972's *Carry on Abroad* and in *Carry On Girls* the following year, when he also made his London stage debut in *The Mating Game*.

His 1976 one-man show *Lauder*, based on the life of his hero, proved a great success, and many more theatre roles followed.

Jimmy was awarded an honorary doctorate by Glasgow Caledonian University in 1994, an OBE for his services to Scottish theatre in 1996 and was elected a Fellow of the Royal Scottish Academy of Music and Drama in 1998.

Jimmy's final performance was in March 2001 at the Glasgow Pavilion, where a who's who of Scottish show business paid tribute to the veteran performer.

Long-term Helensburgh resident Jimmy served as the first honorary president of Helensburgh Heritage Trust until his death on April 13 2001 aged 73.

Ronald Low

GP and Oor Wullie
(1927 – 1992)

The staff at publishers DC Thomson were struggling for inspiration for a new comic strip character when an eight-year-old boy with scruffy hair walked into his father's office, dressed in dungarees and clutching a bucket of potatoes – and a Scottish icon was born.

Ronald Watterston Duncan Low was born on April 21 1927 in Dundee.

His father, RD Low, worked as Head of Children's Publications for publisher DC Thomson, and was keen to launch a lighter comic title aimed at children - he just needed a character. Young Ron's timely visit to his father's office in 1935 led to him being sketched by illustrator Dudley D Watkins whilst sat atop his upturned bucket, and *Oor Wullie* was born. The character first appeared in print in the eight-page *Fun Section* of *The Sunday Post* in March 1936.

Ron attended Dundee High School and St Andrews University, where he studied medicine and was an active participant in the local Air Cadets and University Flying Club.

On graduating from University, and after completing his national service with the Royal Air Force, Ron embarked on a successful career as a GP in Lochinver, Sutherland and married Elsie Sturrock in April 1952.

Ron and his wife then emigrated to Canada where Ron joined the RCAF, training as a jet pilot at RCAF Gimli in Manitoba. Having reached the rank of Squadron Leader and with his flying days behind him, he remained with the RCAF, serving at the Institute of Aviation Medicine and continuing his medical career as a distinguished surgeon.

The couple returned to Scotland in 1977 when Ron was appointed Chief of Occupational Health at Raigmore Hospital in Inverness. Ron and Elsie lived in the Highlands until 1985, when Elsie sadly passed away and Ron retired.

He moved to Helensburgh in 1989 and married the recently widowed Mary Dutch, who had also studied at St. Andrews in the late 1940s. The couple spent time travelling and visiting friends and family until Ron passed away in Helensburgh aged 64 on February 10 1992.

A deeply modest man, Ron's *Oor Wullie* connection was only revealed after his death.

Zachary Macaulay

Statistician & Slavery Abolitionist
(1768 – 1838)

Zachary Macaulay was born on May 2 1768 in Inveraray, the third son of Church of Scotland Minister Rev. John Macaulay and his second wife, Margaret. The family moved to Cardross in May 1774, when John was appointed Minister at the Parish Church.

Although Zachary attended school in the area, he was largely self-taught, becoming proficient in Latin, Greek and English Literature. At fourteen he went to work in a merchant's office in Glasgow, where his boisterous lifestyle convinced him of the need to leave Scotland in 1784.

Aged just 16, Zachary took up a bookkeeping position on a sugar plantation in Jamaica. Although he soon settled down and even excelled in his work, over time he became uneasy about the treatment of plantation slaves.

In 1789, Zachary returned to Britain, taking up a position in London. He often visited his sister Jean and her husband Thomas Babington at their estate in Leicestershire, and became influenced by their circle of friends, which included Henry Thornton and William Wilberforce.

In 1790, through his association with his brother-in-law Babington, Zachary set sail for Sierra Leone, a colony created for emancipated slaves. He became Governor in March 1794, a position he held until 1799.

Returning to London, and to support his family, Zachary became secretary of the Sierra Leone Company until 1808 when the colony was transferred to the British crown. Zachary was elected a member of the Society for the Abolition of the Slave Trade in 1804, where his personal experiences, forensic accounting skills and brilliant analytical mind made him a leading figure in the parliamentary campaign to abolish slavery. During this period Zachary also edited the highly influential magazine *Anti-Slavery Monthly Reporter.*

Zachary never stopped campaigning and, despite failing business interests and ill health, was instrumental in the eventual abolition of slavery throughout the British Empire.

Zachary Macaulay died on May 13 1838 and was buried in Mecklenburgh Square in London. Two months later it was agreed at a meeting led by leading social reformer Sir Thomas Foxwell Buxton MP, to erect a memorial to Macaulay in Westminster Abbey.

David MacDonald

Film Maker
(1904 – 1983)

David was born in Helensburgh on May 9 1904. In his twenties he managed a rubber plantation in Malaya, where one story suggests he met actor Douglas Fairbanks, who suggested that David should try his luck in Hollywood.

He travelled to the USA in 1929, and found work as a technical advisor on the 1932 film *Prestige*, which was partly set in Malaya. Director Cecil B. DeMille then hired him as a production assistant on his 1934 Malayan jungle adventure *Four Frightened People*. David moved to Paramount studios with DeMille in 1932 and worked with a number of other directors before returning to the UK in 1936.

He made his directorial debut with 1937's *Double Alibi,* a low-budget B movie that was part of a series of films known as 'Quota Quickies' that were intended to help stimulate the ailing UK film industry. A number of 'Quickies' were to follow before David had his first taste of success with comedy thriller *This Man is News* in 1938. The film – although technically another Quota movie – was well received, and its three stars Alastair Sim, Barry K Barnes and Valerie Hobson reunited with director David for a sequel *This Man in Paris* in 1939.

During World War II David commanded the Crown Film Unit, where he was responsible for producing two Roy Boulting directed documentaries *Desert Victory* and *Burma Victory.*

David stated that Desert Victory was a "pure, true documentary of the fighting men of the British Army." Winston Churchill was impressed; sending personal copies to World Leaders in March 1943.

After the war, David directed three films for Producer Sydney Box before two big-budget flops put a dent in his career. 1949's *The Bad Lord Byron* and *Christopher Columbus* did so badly at the box office that David's career never really recovered.

The 1950s saw a mini-resurgence of sorts with three films - *Cairo Road* in 1950, 1954's cult classic *Devil Girl From Mars* and 1958's *The Moonraker* - clawing back some prestige. His final film was 1962's *The Golden Rabbit,* after which David worked mostly in television.

David died in London on June 22 1983 at the age of 79.

Helen MacInnes

Author
(1907 – 1985)

Whilst on her honeymoon in Bavaria in 1932, this future writer was disturbed by the activities of the Nazi party and made many notes of the violent acts she witnessed daily. Nine years later these scribblings would form the basis of the plot for her first bestselling novel.

Helen Clark MacInnes was born on October 7 1907 in Glasgow to parents Donald and Jessica. She attended Helensburgh's Hermitage School and then Glasgow High School for Girls.

After graduating with an M.A. from Glasgow University in 1928, Helen received her diploma in librarianship from University College, London. Between 1929 and 1930, she was selector of county library book acquisitions for the Dunbartonshire Education Authority, and it was during this period she met classics scholar Gilbert Highet. The couple married on September 22 1932.

In 1939 the couple left Oxford and settled in New York City. Records suggest Gilbert led a double life as both MI6 British intelligence agent and a classics scholar, his lifestyle proving a significant influence on the subject matter of Helen's writing.

Helen made her breakthrough with her novel *Above Suspicion,* written in 1941 and based largely upon the notes made during her honeymoon. An instant best seller, the book quickly became a film starring Joan Crawford and Fred MacMurray in 1943.

Her second novel, 1942's *Assignment in Brittany* was considered valuable research for Allied intelligence agents working with the French Resistance, and the portrayal of Polish resistance in her 1944 book *The Unconquerable* was considered to be so accurate that it was alleged she was using classified information passed to her by her husband.

Helen's 21 novels, usually featuring complex political plots in which communist forces pose security threats, have been translated into 22 languages and have sold millions of copies around the globe, leading to her title as 'The Queen of the Spy Writers'.

Helen became a naturalised American citizen in 1951; in 1966 her work was formally recognised when she was awarded the Columba Prize in Literature by New York's Iona College.

Helen passed away on 30 September 30 1985 in New York at the age of 77.

William de Bois Maclaren

Businessman & Scouting Movement Benefactor (1856 – 1921)

Gilwell Park, the training and camping centre on the edge of Epping Forest, is a major focal point for the Scouting movement throughout the world, a site that owes its existence to a businessman from Rosneath.

William Frederick de Bois Maclaren was born on 17 November 1856, in Blythswood, Glasgow, the second child of master printer Walter Gray Maclaren and his French wife Caroline Amelia De Bois.

A talented writer, William followed his father into the print business, dividing his time between the London and Glasgow offices of the family publishing company Maclaren & Sons, which he managed together with partner Frank Copeman.

In 1892, aged 35, William married Anna Jane White and the couple moved to Armadale House in Rosneath.

Maclaren & Sons output included general trade journals such as *The British Baker and Confectioner* and *The India Rubber Journal*, a publication that convinced Maclaren and Copeman of the commercial opportunities offered by rubber.

In 1906 they founded the Rubber Estate Agency Limited, the UK's first company established to represent and finance companies involved with rubber cultivation. This venture, which in 1913 also led William to write the definitive book on the subject, *The Rubber Tree Book*, made him a very wealthy man.

William, himself a Dunbartonshire District Scout Commissioner, often visited London's East End on business and was saddened to see that Scouts in the area lacked a suitable outdoor space in which to conduct their activities. In November 1918 he met with Robert Baden-Powell, founder of The Boy Scouts Association, to discuss the purchase of a permanent camping ground for London Scouts.

A suitable site at was found at Gilwell Park, with William donating the then substantial sum of £10,000 towards its purchase and development. At the official opening on July 26 1919, William was awarded the Silver Wolf, the Scouting movement's highest honour, by Baden-Powell.

In a continuing debt of gratitude, Scouters in over 120 countries who have been awarded the Wood Badge wear a neckerchief that features a swatch of Maclaren tartan at its point.

William died at Rosneath on June 3 1921 aged 64.

Maud MacLellan OBE

Corps Commander FANY
(1903 – 1977)

An instruction from the War Office in March 1945 - to make arrangements to train 'a very important person as a motor car driver and in motor mechanics' - led to a Helensburgh resident organising driving lessons for the future Queen.

Maud Lilburn MacLellan was born on October 6 1903 in Glasgow to Walter Thomas MacLellan and his wife, Jane Adair Whyte. Later that year, the family moved to Helensburgh's Sinclair Street.

In 1929 Maud joined the Glasgow section of the First Aid Nursing Yeomanry. Created in 1907 FANY represented a first aid link between front-line fighting units and field hospitals.

FANY had been expanding its recruitment since the end of WW1, and as the storm clouds of WWII gathered, its role evolved to include the provision of cooks, drivers, communications specialists and clerks to the Army, RAF and SOE. It was thus well placed to supply the first 1500 driver/mechanics to the newly formed women's Auxiliary Territorial Service (ATS) in 1938.

Although promised autonomy within the ATS, many existing FANY personnel were forced into enrolling into the fledgling service, leaving many feeling bitter and betrayed.

In a move designed to overcome hostility toward the new women's service, Maud, by now a senior FANY officer, accepted command of the 4th Scottish Motor Company ATS in 1938, taking overall Command of the Motor Transport Training Centre at Camberley in 1940.

During this period Maud oversaw the training of HRH Princess Elizabeth who, as a regular junior officer, learned to drive a utility vehicle, an ambulance and a saloon car.

Maud returned to the FANY after the war and became Corps Commander in 1947, a post she held until her retirement in 1965. In 1957, the Corps' fiftieth anniversary year, Maud was awarded the OBE for her life of service.

Maud died on May 21 1977 at 9 East Abercrombie Street, Helensburgh, having spent much of her retirement pursuing her passion for angling.

In 1999 the Commandant in Chief, HRH the Princess Royal, gave the Corps permission to use her title and is now known as FANY (The Princess Royal's Volunteer Corps).

Murdo MacLeod

Footballer & Broadcaster

Murdo Davidson MacLeod was born in Milngavie on September 24 1958.

A long-time resident of Helensburgh, Murdo will always be remembered – particularly on the West Coast - for his extremely successful footballing career.

He first made his name with Dumbarton in 1974 before moving to Celtic in 1978, one year after marrying Mhairi in Jamestown Parish Church, and five years before settling in Helensburgh.

During his nine years at Celtic he helped the club to five league titles, two Scottish Cups and one League Cup. Murdo also has the distinction of scoring the greatest ever Old Firm goal as voted by Celtic supporters in a 2000 poll, the goal in question helping Celtic win the 1979 league championship in a decisive match against Rangers FC.

The first of his 20 Scotland caps was awarded against England in the 1985 Rous Cup. Murdo would represent his country at the 1990 World Cup in Italy, where he was famously knocked unconscious by a 90 mph free kick taken by Brazilian Branco.

In 1987 Murdo moved from Celtic to German club Borussia Dortmund, the first Scot to pull on the famous yellow and black strip, where he played over 100 games in four years, winning two major trophies.

He returned to Scotland with Hibernian, where he captained the club to a League Cup win in 1991.

After a successful playing career, he returned to Dumbarton as player-coach, guiding them to promotion from Division Two with a last-gasp victory over Stirling Albion in 1995.

In the summer of 1995, he left the Sons to manage Partick Thistle, his tenure at Firhill ending in relegation at the end of the 1995-96 season. In 1997 he returned to Celtic as assistant coach under Wim Jansen, helping the club win their first league title in 9 years; the pair also won the League Cup double during their only season in charge.

On leaving Celtic, Murdo commenced a thriving media career. He continues to write for national newspapers, and regularly appears on television and radio as both analyst and commentator.

Away from sport, Murdo a devoted family man, has enjoyed running several successful businesses.

Dr Osborne Henry Mavor CBE

Playwright & Surgeon
(1888 – 1951)

Osborne Henry Mavor was born in Glasgow on January 3 1888.

Following his education at Glasgow Academy, he spent ten years studying medicine at Glasgow University, eventually graduating as a Bachelor of Medicine and Surgery in 1913.

Upon graduation, Osborne worked as a house physician and surgeon at the Glasgow Royal Infirmary. At the outbreak of World War 1, he enlisted in the Royal Army Medical Corps and within three months was serving in France.

In 1917 he was sent out to the Middle East and served in Mesopotamia, India, Persia and Constantinople. It was whilst stationed in these countries that he collected many stories that would eventually surface in his plays.

The career for which Osborne is best known had already begun to take shape by 1928, when his first play was produced. *The Sunlight Sonata* was written under the pseudonym Mary Henderson. He adopted another pseudonym, James Bridie, for his subsequent works, finding his first major success with 1930s *The Anatomist,* based on Victorian vivisectionist Dr Robert Knox.

In 1934, Osborne left his medical career to concentrate on the theatre. He gave up his practise and moved his family to a house – Rockbank - at 150 East Clyde Street in Helensburgh.

Osborne's success continued throughout the 1930s and 40s; writing some 40 plays as Bridie and in the late 1940s he moved into screenwriting, collaborating with director Alfred Hitchcock on films such as *The Paradine Case, Under Capricorn* and *Stage Fright.*

There can be no doubt as to Osborne's importance to the Scottish Arts scene. He took the lead in the establishment of the Glasgow Citizens' Theatre in 1943 and in 1950 helped found the College of Drama in Glasgow, later to become the Royal Scottish Academy of Music and Drama. He was also a Director of the Scottish National Theatre Society and chairman of the Scottish committee of the Council for the Encouragement of Music and the Arts, an organisation that was the precursor of the Arts Council.

He died in Edinburgh Royal Infirmary on January 29 1951 and is buried in Glasgow's Western Necropolis.

Daniel McCoshan

Tenor
(1920 – 2003)

Daniel McCoshan was born in Helensburgh in 1920, and grew up to be a popular and familiar figure locally. He lost his left eye in an accident at the age of six but this disability did not hamper his path to success in later life.

Blessed with an extraordinary voice, Daniel sang regularly as a choirboy and in various local amateur dramatics productions. A beautiful rendition of Handel's *Messiah* at Helensburgh's St. Michael's Church was particularly well received.

In 1940, Daniel was called up, and served with the Black Watch and later the Pioneer Corps. Placed in charge of Italian Prisoners of War at Ledbury, Daniel soon learned to speak Italian, a skill that would benefit him greatly in later life.

After the war, he worked as a gardener with the Parks' Department in Helensburgh, and it was during this period that he was asked to reprise his *Messiah* performance.

Such was the power and emotion of Daniel's voice, a member of the audience suggested he should consider a professional singing career. Despite Daniel's polite protestations that this could never happen, several members of the community secretly organised an audition for him at the Guildhall School of Music. Daniel, by now in his early thirties, was accepted as a student, winning the coveted Gold Medal for Tenor voice in his first year.

Following his graduation from the Guildhall in the mid 1950s, Daniel joined the Glyndebourne Opera before signing a contract in 1961 with Royal Opera House in Covent Garden where he stayed for thirty years as a member of the chorus.

Although Daniel spent his singing career in England, he never forgot his Helensburgh roots, returning regularly to visit his family and to perform at Burns Suppers throughout Scotland. On one such visit in 1963, Daniel sang two Hymns for the BBC's *Songs of Praise,* recorded at Helensburgh's Old & St. Andrew's Parish Church.

During a distinguished career, Daniel sang with many of the great names of Opera from the Three Tenors to Joan Sutherland and Kiri Takanawa.

He died aged 82 in Kidderminster Hospital on January 21 2003.

Gus McCuaig

Sportsman

A former Rhu Amateurs' footballer became the first man to represent Scotland in both track and racquet sports.

Angus McCuaig was born on January 7 1958 in Garelochhead to Archie, a local school janitor, and wife Violet. He attended the local primary school and Helenburgh's Hermitage Academy before embarking on a career as a plumbing and heating engineer.

After a stint with Rhu Amateurs, earning praise for his speed as a player, Gus was introduced to Charlie Affleck, coach to Olympic Champion Alan Wells, and the pair began to work together.

In 1981, Gus entered the New Year Powderhall 110m Sprint at Meadowbank, winning the race in a record time of 10.55 seconds, the first West of Scotland runner to do so for nearly 50 years. In collecting the £1000 winner's cheque, Gus inadvertently forfeited his amateur status, which technically prevented him from representing his country in the future. He successfully appealed the decision, donating the winnings to the Amateur Athletics Association (AAA) and giving up his job in order to concentrate on athletics full time.

Gus won his first amateur race in June 1981, the 200m at the Scottish AAA championships, a race he would go on to win a record five times in a row. In 1982 he represented both Scotland and Team GB for the first time, winning individual 100m, 200m and Sprint Relay gold and silver medals at various meets.

In the autumn of 1982, Gus, along with Alan Wells, Cameron Sharp and Drew McMaster represented Scotland in the 4 x 100m relay at the Brisbane Commonwealth Games, returning with a bronze medal.

Over the next few years, Gus travelled the globe, competing at all the major championships - a member of Team GB's golden age of sprinters alongside Linford Christie, John Regis and Mike McFarlane - until a cruciate injury forced his retirement in the late 1980s.

However, the end of his track career did not end his life as a top sportsman. A long-time member of Cameron House Squash Club, Gus progressed through the rankings to represent Scotland in the Over 45s Masters series.

Alex McCuaig

Experiential Designer

As a 16 year old living beside the Clyde, Alex McCuaig witnessed the launch of the QE2 in September 1967 with a mixture of excitement and awe, little realising that some forty years later he would lead the public space design team as the ship entered her second life as a luxury floating hotel.

Alex was born in Glasgow on July 12 1951 to Archie and Violet McCuaig. One of four sons – brother Gus represented TeamGB in athletics – Alex attended Garelochhead Primary School and Helensburgh's Hermitage Academy.

After leaving school and doing a variety of jobs, Alex studied Fine Art at Goldsmiths, University of London and 3D Design at Kingston University, where his degree show caught the attention of James G Gardner – then Britain's most successful exhibition designer – who promptly offered him a job.

His apprenticeship with Gardner lasted four years, after which Alex felt confident enough to start his own design practice. In 1982, he founded MET Studio in London, its first major project being a collaboration with Gardner for the National Museum of Natural Science in Taiwan.

Over the years, MET Studio has worked with some of the world's leading museums, information centres, zoos, eco parks and brands in more than 50 countries, delivering projects ranging from large-scale masterplans to one-off installations.

The Studio and its projects have won many major awards for both innovation and commerce including an International Trade Queens Award for Enterprise, National Heritage Museum of the Year, Exporter of the Year, and International Interior Design of the Year.

In 2016, MET Studio won Design Week & IBM's *Age of Design Award* for Best Design work over the past 25 years for its *Wired Worlds* exhibition at the National Museum of Photography, Film & Television in Bradford, beating design heavyweights including the Apple iPhone, Norton F1 motorcycle and even the BBC in the process.

Alex was personally recognised for his thirty-year contribution to the design of educational, cultural and immersive brand experiences by being presented with an award for Outstanding Lifetime Contribution to Design at the 2016 FX International Design Awards.

Vice Admiral Sir Ian McGeoch
KCB DSO DSC

Royal Navy Officer
(1914 – 2007)

Ian Lachlan Mackay McGeoch was born on March 26 1914 in Helensburgh, where he was inspired to pursue a life at sea by messing about in boats on the Firth of Clyde.

He was educated at Pangbourne, and entered the Royal Navy as a special entry cadet in 1931.

In 1933 he served as a midshipman on the battleship *Royal Oak*, the destroyer Boadicea and the cruiser *Devonshire*, but six years later began to specialise in submarines.

On the outbreak of war Ian was third hand in the submarine *Clyde*. In 1940 after passing the demanding Commanding Officers' Qualifying Course, he was sent to Malta as spare commanding officer. Ian took command of HMS *Ursula* for one patrol, but elected to return to England and take the qualification again before taking command of a new S class submarine HMS *Splendid* in January 1942.

Under his command *Splendid* sank more tonnage on its six patrols than any other submarine. Ian was awarded the DSO after his fourth patrol, and the DSC after his fifth. But his luck changed on April 21 1943 when the German destroyer Hermes depth-charged Splendid. 18 crew were lost, and Ian was blinded in his right eye. All the survivors – including Ian - were sent to an Italian POW camp.

Ian eventually escaped and made his way back to Britain. He attended the naval staff course in 1944 and became staff officer operations in the 4th Cruiser Squadron of the British Pacific Fleet.

After World War II Ian continued to serve and was promoted several times before becoming vice-admiral in 1967. He was appointed CB in 1966 and KCB in 1969 before retiring from the Navy in 1970.

Enrolling at Edinburgh University he studied Social Sciences, receiving an MPhil in 1975 for his thesis on the origins, procurement and effect of the *Polaris* nuclear programme. Between 1972 and 1980 he was editor of *The Naval Review.*

Ian was also a member of the Queen's Body Guard for Scotland, the Royal Company of Archers and of the Royal Yacht Squadron.

He died on August 12 2007 aged 93.

Bobby McGregor MBE

Swimmer

Forever known as the 'Falkirk Flyer', Bobby McGregor followed in his father's footsteps by competing in the pool at a Summer Olympics.

Robert Bilsand McGregor was born in Glasgow on April 3 1944 to parents David and Nancy. The family moved to Helensburgh shortly after he was born before relocating to Falkirk when Bobby was three.

As Falkirk's baths master, Bobby's father, who was a member of the British 1936 Berlin Olympics water polo squad, was anxious to teach McGregor junior to swim. Bobby had his first swimming lesson at the age of nine – and won his first championship, the Falkirk Primary Schools title, a year later.

It was the start of a glittering career that would see him earn international recognition as one of the best swimmers of his generation.

Bobby first represented Scotland aged 16 as part of the squad competing for the Tenovus Cup at the Empire Pool in Cardiff in 1960.

In August 1964 he set a world record with a sensational swim in the 110 yards final at the British Championships to win in 53.6 seconds. Later the same day he was named captain of the British Olympic swimming team to compete at the Tokyo Games, where he went on to win a silver medal.

After his success in Tokyo, Bobby attended a lunch at Buckingham Palace, where the Queen told him: "I watched your race on television. It was very exciting and if you'd had a longer finger you would have won".

In 1966, in the space of five weeks, Bobby won a Commonwealth Games silver medal and a European Championships gold medal, then broke his own world record for the 110 yards at the British Championships. It was at the end of this remarkable year that Bobby was awarded the MBE by the Queen for services to sport.

Bobby retired from competitive swimming after the 1968 Olympics, aged 24, with a fourth place finish in the 100 metres freestyle final, and returned to Helensburgh in the late 1980s.

In 2002 he was one of the first sportsmen to be inducted into the Scottish Sports Hall of Fame.

Emeritus Professor Alasdair McIntyre
CBE DSc FRSE

Marine Biologist
(1926 – 2010)

Exploring the rock pools on the banks of the Clyde led this young boy to become a central figure in Scottish marine biology for over forty years.

Alasdair Duncan McIntyre, CBE, DSc, FRSE was born in Helensburgh on November 17 1926.

He was educated at Hermitage School in Helensburgh and at Glasgow University, graduating in 1949 with first class honours in Zoology.

In 1951, he joined the Marine Laboratory in Aberdeen, where he was to remain for 36 years. It was there that he met his wife, Catherine, after she started work as an administrator in 1964. The couple married in 1967 at Aberdeen's Craigiebuckler Church.

During his career at the Laboratory, Alasdair conducted and led research on marine ecology, fisheries and pollution. Such was his eminence he also became chairman of the United Nations Joint Group of Experts on Scientific Aspects of Marine Pollution and advised the International Council for the Exploration of the Sea on marine pollution.

He was awarded a DSc by Glasgow University in 1970 for his thesis on Marine Benthic Ecology and was elected a Fellow of the Royal Society of Edinburgh the following year before becoming a Fellow of the Institute of Biology in 1980.

He was appointed director of Fisheries Research for Scotland in 1983 and Co-Ordinator of Fisheries Research and Development for the UK in 1986. He retired from the Marine Laboratory aged 60 in 1987 and was made Emeritus Professor of Fisheries and Oceanography at Aberdeen University.

Alasdair was deeply involved in issues of marine environmental quality and human impact, including the effects of fishing, pollutants and oil exploitation. In 2003, he advised the fishing industry and the Government to find a compromise when the Government proposed a No Fishing Zone off the north coast of Scotland. His contribution to marine conservation and fisheries was recognised in June 1994 when he was appointed CBE.

In his spare time Alasdair was an enthusiastic supporter of Aberdeen Football Club, and was a connoisseur of food, wine and malt whisky.

Alasdair died in Aberdeen on 15th April 15 2010 at the age of 83.

Mike McIntyre MBE

Yachtsman

Michael Mackay McIntyre was born on June 29 1956 in Glasgow to eminent veterinary scientist Professor Ian McIntyre and his wife Ruth.

Mike's Father had left the UK in 1963 to take a select team of colleagues from Glasgow to inaugurate a school of veterinary surgery at the newly established University of East Africa in Nairobi.

In 1968 Professor McIntyre returned to Scotland to the Glasgow Veterinary School, and the family moved into a house in Stuckenduff, Shandon.

Once settled back in Scotland, Mike attended Hermitage Academy. As a naturally keen sportsman, Ian encouraged his sons to 'take to the Clyde' and sail.

Mike became a Scottish Schools swimming champion at the age of 12 and went on to become an extremely talented yachtsman.

After more than six years of training, Mike sailed a Finn class dinghy at the 1984 Los Angeles Olympics finishing in seventh place. Four years later at the 1988 Seoul Olympics, partnering Philip Bryn Vaile in the Star Class, Mike went on to win Gold for Team GB. The British boat won gold by 11 seconds with a total of 45.7 points.

Mike graduated from University of Glasgow in 1977, BSc in Electronic and Electrical Engineering, and away from the water, has spent his working life in the IT and technology sectors, having worked with Orbitel, Call Sciences Ltd and Dolphin Telecom. He has led major change and performance improvement programmes for clients such as RAC, Virgin, and Vodafone. In 2002, Mike co-founded IT Consultancy firm Xenogenix in Surrey.

In June 2012, Mike made his return to the competitive arena when he entered the Skandia Sail for Gold Regatta, partnering Hayling Island sailing club friend James Grant for the one-off event. Unfortunately Mike's comeback ended early when he and Grant collided with John Gimson and Robert Shanks during a race on day two. The collision left a gaping hole in Mike's boat, which ironically belonged to Gimson.

Mike now lives at Hayling Island in Hampshire where he is an active member of the local Sailing Club; however he remains the Honorary Commodore of Helensburgh Sailing Club and still sails under its burgee.

Emeritus Professor Ian McIntyre
CBE PHD FRCVS

Veterinary Teacher
(1919 – 2008)

A request from a head of state led this academic from the West Coast of Scotland to the West Coast of Africa to undertake ground breaking veterinary research.

William Ian Mackay McIntyre was born on July 7 1919, in Altnaharra, Sutherland, the son of a gamekeeper. It was the time spent walking his dogs with his father on the Kimball estate in Sutherland that led to Ian's early interest in animals and wildlife.

He was educated in Altnaharra and Golspie but unfortunately on his last day at school he suffered a road accident that led to a year in hospital with serious leg injuries. During his convalescence his father died. The estate owner supported Ian's desire to study veterinary medicine, an act of generosity which Ian never forgot.

Ian continued his studies, graduating BVMS from the Royal Veterinary School in Edinburgh in 1944. After graduation he remained on the staff and ran the small animal clinic, writing a PhD thesis on canine bacterial infections. It was during this period that Ian married his first wife, Ruth Galbraith, in 1948.

Three years later Ian was recruited by Professor William Weipers to lead the department of veterinary medicine at the Glasgow Veterinary School. He was appointed Professor of Veterinary Medicine in 1961.

In 1963 Ian took a select team of colleagues from Glasgow to inaugurate a school of veterinary surgery at the newly established University of East Africa in Nairobi.

Ian returned to the Glasgow Veterinary School in 1968, and he and his wife Ruth, and their three sons Peter, Mike and John, moved into a house in Stuckenduff, Shandon.

In the early 1970's, he was invited by Gambian President Sir Dawda Jawarra – himself a former Glasgow veterinary graduate - to help identify the effects of trypanosomiasis on the local cattle stock. Ian's work in Africa was formally recognised when he was appointed CBE in 1989 for services to veterinary research in the Gambia.

After his final retirement in 1989, Ian spent time touring his beloved Highlands.

Ian married his second wife Elizabeth in 2007 but sadly died at home in Shandon on March 20 the following year at the age of 88.

Steve McLaughlin

Musician & Producer

Some of the most memorable movie and television scores of the past few decades, including the Die Hard and Lethal Weapon series and the Oscar-nominated scores for *Interview with the Vampire* and Michael Collins have been produced, recorded and mixed by a talented musician from Helensburgh.

Stephen McLaughlin was born October 25 1960 in Helensburgh, where he grew up in Craigendoran and attended Hermitage Academy.

Steve's musical career began as the drummer with the late '70s punk group The Cubs, part of the post-punk scene in Edinburgh that also featured bands such as The Fire Engines and Joseph K.

In 1980, Steve joined Scars and participated in the recording of the band's only LP, 1981's critically acclaimed *Author! Author!* After the band split in 1982, Steve headed to London and became a recording engineer at Zomba's Battery Studios.

In 1987, he was approached by composer Michael Kamen to work on the score for Ridley Scott's film *Someone to Watch Over Me*. It was to be the start of a fifteen-year working partnership for the pair that included producing Kamen's score for 1991's *Robin Hood: Prince of Thieves,* with the resulting soundtrack album going on to sell 3.5 million copies.

Another commercial hit followed a year later, when they co-produced Sting's single *It's Probably Me* for the film *Lethal Weapon 3,* with it reaching number one in several countries. Over the years Steve has produced, recorded and mixed the scores for more than 150 feature films, working with directors such as Francis Ford Coppola, Robert Altman, Michael Mann and Brad Bird.

In 1995 Steve's talent was recognised when he received a Grammy Award for Best Engineered Album (Non Classical) for his work on Tom Petty's *Wildflowers* album. He has also received two Motion Picture Sound Editors Golden Reel Awards for Best Scoring Mixer.

In 1999, Stephen formed the production company gohlmcLaughlin with fellow music producer Teese Gohl. The company, which continues to produce scores for films as diverse as *Stardust, Hannibal Rising* and *The Young Victoria*, specialises in working with writers and composers who are new to the film scoring process.

Lex McLean

Music Hall & Variety Performer
(1907 – 1975)

Alexander McLean Cameron was born on April 30 1907 in Clydebank, son of Donald and his second wife, Mary.

Whilst his parents hoped that he would become a classical musician and attend university, they were to be disappointed on both counts. Lex was expelled from school and abandoned his piano lessons in favour of the accordion. He was so scared to tell his mother that he fled to Belfast with just £4 in his pocket. In turn, his parents were telling anyone who enquired about their son that he was on the road as a commercial traveller, such was the stigma attached to touring 'theatrical types'.

Lex spent time busking, touring with variety shows and working as a foil to other comedians before finally embarking on a solo career in 1947.

He finally achieved star billing in 1955 when he succeeded Tommy Morgan as host of the Pavilion Theatre Glasgow's summer shows, which won him a steadily increasing following.

Wearing a red cloak and top hat, or a flat cap and baggy trousers, his act was rich in comedy innuendo, peppered with a host of catchphrases, most notably "Keep it bright, keep it bright!."

Even though he was dubbed 'Sexy Lexy' due to the suggestive nature of his act and 'patter', his material was passed as being 'suitable for the public' by the Lord Chamberlain and Glaswegians queued in their thousands to see him.

Away from the theatre, Lex was a very quiet and private man. His home, purchased in 1959, was a beautiful Villa on the sea front in Helensburgh, where he lived with wife Grace, a former dancer he'd met during a summer season at Burntisland.

After each show at the Pavilion, Lex would dash out of the stage door and run down to Queen Street Station to catch the last train to Helensburgh, usually reaching home at three minutes past midnight. During each day he would sit writing new material in his rocking chair, facing beautiful views of the Clyde Estuary.

Lex passed away at his beloved home in Cumberland Avenue in Helensburgh on March 23 1975.

Moses McNeil

Football Pioneer
(1855 – 1938)

Moses McNeil was born on October 29 1855 at Belmore House in Rhu to parents John and Jean. His father was gardener at Belmore, the summer retreat of Glasgow corn merchant John Honeyman.

Moses grew up in the Helensburgh area until the end of 1871, when he followed his brothers and sister to Glasgow.

In early March 1872, inspired by seeing Queens Park play, Moses, his brother Peter, and friends William McBeath and Peter Campbell discussed forming a football team whilst walking in Glasgow's West End Park, now known as Kelvingrove.

The team that the men went on to form was Glasgow Rangers, allegedly named after a prominent English Rugby team of the era, Swindon Rangers, who had featured in a copy of a sporting annual Moses had been reading at the time.

Rangers played their first ever match against Callender F.C. at Glasgow Green's Flesher's Haugh in May 1872, resulting in a 0-0 draw. Rangers played one further match in 1872, an 11-0 win against Clyde.

The team won their first trophy in 1879, The Glasgow Merchants' Charity Cup, after beating Vale of Leven 2-1 in front of 11,000 spectators at Hampden. The team won its first Scottish Cup after a 3–1 win over Celtic in 1894.

Moses would win two caps for Scotland, and was the first Ranger to represent his country.

His last recorded appearance for Rangers was on September 30, 1882 in a Scottish Cup replay defeat to Queen's Park at Hampden.

After his footballing career ended, Moses spent much of his working life as a clerk, and later a commercial traveller, for Hugh Lang Junior, a commission agent based at 70 Union Street in Glasgow.

In 1930, Moses moved back to the Helensburgh area when he moved into his sister Isabella's cottage in Rosneath, where he was to spend the rest of his life.

Moses, who never married, died on April 9 1938, aged 82. He was buried in Rosneath graveyard, sharing a grave with his sisters Isabella and Elizabeth and her husband Duncan Gray. Sadly his name was never added to the family gravestone but in June 2015 fans of the club unveiled a plaque to commemorate Moses' last resting place.

Fergus McNeill

Games Developer & Author

Fergus McNeill was born to parents Marian and Duncan McNeill in February 1969. Although born in Glasgow, Fergus grew up in Helensburgh and lived in the town until 1975 when the family moved to Fintry.

When he was 11, Fergus' family moved to Hampshire, where he attended Swanmore Secondary School. It was around this time that his parents thought there would be "no harm" in buying him a Sinclair ZX81 computer.

Fergus began creating and writing games in his spare time when he was just 14. He took Computer Studies O Level at School, creating a text adventure in BASIC as his course project. Fergus displayed an early entrepreneurial spirit and began selling games via mail order under the Delta 4 brand.

Over the following years he became well known in the Gaming industry, both for his own content and for his adaptations of other authors' material, notably his collaboration with Terry Pratchett to create the first Discworld game.

During his career Fergus has designed, directed and illustrated games for all sorts of systems, working with companies such as CRL, Silversoft, Macmillan Group, Activision, SCi Eidos and EA.

Fergus set up and managed the development studio for SCi - now Eidos - where he co-wrote and directed voiceover scripts for a number of games including the award-winning *Kingdom O' Magic* and co-produced titles including the infamous *Carmageddon.*

In 2005, he joined InfoSpace to manage their mobile games studio, and then worked with colleagues to conclude a successful management buy out, re-launching the studio as FinBlade in 2007. The company's clients have included Nissan, BMW, Red Bull Racing, Liverpool FC and Peter Gabriel.

Fergus continues to develop games and apps for phones, tablets, and social media platforms, but is also focused on his second career as an author.

His first novel, the contemporary thriller *Eye Contact,* was published in 2012, and he has since written a further two novels *Knife Edge, Cut Out* and a novella *Broken Fall.*

He is a founder member of TIGA, the trade association for the UK Gaming Industry, and is a member of the Crime Writers' Association and BAFTA.

Commander Peter Meryon DSC

Royal Navy Officer
(1920 – 2005)

Remembered as the first naval officer in the Second World War to retrieve secret documents from an enemy submarine, this Helensburgh born officer spent his life serving his country.

Peter Louis Meryon was born in Helensburgh on June 27 1920. At the age of 13 he attended the Royal Naval College in Dartmouth, becoming the third generation of his family to serve in the Royal Navy.

Prior to World War II Peter served as a midshipman on the battleship *Malaya*, which took part in the bombardment of the French fleet at Mers el Kebir. The ship also escorted convoys in both the Mediterranean and the Atlantic.

On October 18 1940 the Italian submarine *Durbo* was depth-charged to the surface and the crew immediately began to abandon ship. 20-year-old Peter was sub-lieutenant on the destroyer *Wrestler*, which came alongside the *Durbo* and, as the Italian crew were coming up, he led a group down the ladder to *Durbo's* darkened control room, where they retrieved signal books and secret charts by torchlight before abandoning the sinking vessel.

The captured charts revealed the presence of another submarine, *Lafole*, which was hunted and sunk two days later. Peter was awarded a DSC.

By 1944 Peter was first lieutenant of the River class frigate *Nith*, which on June 24 1944 was attacked by a twin-engine unmanned bomber carrying a 3,500-kilogram warhead. Peter's 1988 account of this event was disputed by officials from the Imperial War Museum, who doubted that the Germans possessed such technology in 1944. Later research confirmed that these aircraft did in fact exist at the time.

Peter ended his active service as first lieutenant of *Venus*, one of five fleet destroyers of the 26th Flotilla, which surprised and destroyed the Japanese heavy cruiser *Haguro* and her escorts in a night-time torpedo raid on May 16 1945.

After the war Peter helped train young sailors at HMS Ganges near Ipswich, served on the destroyer *Alamein*, the carrier *Indomitable*, the cruiser *Sheffield* and at the Royal Naval Staff College. His final appointment was to CENTO headquarters in the Turkish capital Ankara.

Peter died in Hampshire on March 9 2005 aged 84.

Neil Mitchell

Musician

With three UK number one records to their credit, fifteen million records sold to date, and tours that have played to over four million people in more than 25 countries, Wet Wet Wet are one of the most successful bands in British pop history.

Neil Mitchell, the group's keyboard player, was born on June 8 1965 in Helensburgh.

The band began in 1977 when a 12-year-old Graeme Clark, a pupil at Clydebank High School, bought his first guitar. A chance meeting with drummer Tommy Cunningham on the school bus led the two to becoming close friends.

The pair approached their mutual school friend Neil, who promised to supply keyboards with money earned from his paper round, to form a group.

Neil recalls: "I actually started on drums, for a week, but Tommy came along and blew me away because I was terrible. I couldn't play guitar either and was a terrible singer, so it had to be keyboards as there wasn't anything else left."

A lead singer was required and Clark approached 16-year-old Mark McLachlan, who tweaked his nickname 'Smarty' adding his mother's maiden name, to become Marti Pellow.

In 1981, with the line-up complete, the band – then known as Vortex Motion - began performing at local clubs. The following year, the band name changed to Wet Wet Wet, a title taken from a Scritti Politti song, and were signed by PolyGram Records in 1985.

The band's first single *Wishing I Was Lucky* was released in 1987, entering the UK Top Ten, with debut album *Popped in Souled Out* reaching number one.

For the next decade the group released a string of hit records and collected many awards, including the 1988 Brit Award for Best British Breakthrough act. In 1994, their version of the Troggs' *Love is All Around* topped the UK singles charts for 15 weeks, and in 1995 the group was officially recognised as the most popular live act in the UK.

The band split at the end of the 90s but the original line-up has reformed on several occasions since then to both perform and record together.

Duncan Muggoch

Film and TV Line Producer

It somehow seems appropriate that the area that gave the world the Father of Television, John Logie Baird, should also have been the childhood home of a man whose production skills have contributed towards one of the most successful TV series of all time – HBO's *Game of Thrones*.

Duncan Muggoch was born in February 1965, raised in Rhu and went to Keil School, Dumbarton.

In 1982, Duncan moved to Glasgow to work for his family's food business – J.W.Galloway Ltd, a major Scottish Meat Company that supplies major retailers - before joining the BBC in 1990. During his time with the corporation he worked within the Design Group in various areas, including Set Design, Costume, Make Up and Special Effects. His final role with the BBC was as Contracts/Production Manager, a position he held between 1994 and 1996.

Duncan left the BBC in 1997 to work freelance as a Location Manager, Unit Production Manager and Line Producer. One of his first projects was as Location Manager for the A&E Television Networks and BBC co-produced television series *Tom Jones – The History of a Foundling*.

Since then, Duncan has been involved with many major feature film and television productions including *The Eagle, Dark Shadows, The Wolfman, Made of Honor, Bourne Ultimatum, The Da Vinci Code, Stardust* and *Still Crazy*.

In 2000, Duncan returned to settle in Rhu and used his expertise and knowledge of Scotland to great effect as Location Manager for the BBC dramas *Rockface* in 2002 and *Monarch of the Glen* between 2002 and 2004.

In addition to his location management roles, Duncan has also scouted locations for films such as *Captain America, Skyfall* and *Charlotte Gray*.

Since 2013, Duncan has supervised all the location filming for *Game of Thrones* outside of Northern Ireland – including locations in Spain and Croatia - as the series' Line Producer.

Duncan was part of the *Game of Thrones* Production team that won the Primetime Emmy in 2015 for Outstanding Drama Series.

Duncan is a full member of the Production Guild of Great Britain and member of the Association of Film and TV Practitioners Scotland.

Neil Munro

Writer & Journalist
(1863 – 1930)

Neil Munro was born the illegitimate son of kitchen maid Ann Munro, on June 3 1863.

He was educated at the parish school in Inveraray until 1877 when he left to take up employment as a clerk in a local lawyer's office. Whilst working there he learned a little Latin and taught himself shorthand.

On the 1st June 1881, two days before his eighteenth birthday, he left Inveraray in search of better prospects. He finally found them in journalism, working as a reporter on the *Greenock Advertiser,* the *Glasgow News,* and the *Falkirk Herald* before finally becoming chief reporter on the *Glasgow Evening News* at the age of only 23. He then married Jessie Adam, the daughter of his landlady in North Woodside Road.

In 1896 he made his literary debut with a collection of stories *The Lost Pibroch and Other Sheiling Stories.* These were soon followed by the release of his first novel *John Splendid* in 1898. He became editor of the *Glasgow Evening News* and was generally regarded as being a senior figure in contemporary Scottish criticism and letters.

Around 1902 Neil retired from full-time journalism, retaining a commitment to produce a weekly column for the *Evening News.* This column won him as much fame as his novels. In it appeared three series of short stories - *Archie, My Droll Friend, Jimmy Swan, the Joy Traveller* and most famously *Para Handy.* The adventures of a West Highland puffer skipper and the crew of the coaster Vital Spark have enjoyed continuing popularity and have been adapted for television, stage and film.

During the World War I Munro returned to full-time journalism but after the loss of his son on the Western Front, his later output was slight.

In 1927 Neil's health was failing and he reluctantly retired from the *Glasgow Evening News.* His last book was a 1928 *History of the Royal Bank of Scotland* and he continued to write articles, *Random Reminiscences* under the pseudonym 'Mr Incognito' for the Daily Record and Mail.

He passed away on December 22 1930 at his home Cromalt on East Clyde Street in Helensburgh.

Paul Murdoch

Author & Musician

'A Terry Pratchett for children and young adults.'

So stated a review of a series of books written by author Paul Murdoch which feature an asthmatic young boy, James Peck, as its hero.

Son of a slater and plasterer, Paul was born in Helensburgh's Braeholm maternity hospital on May 9 1961.

Throughout his childhood, Paul spent many weekends in Helensburgh with his parents walking the pier and braving the chilly outdoor pool. He then went on to study Zoology at Glasgow University between 1979 and 1983, working his way through his university years by playing with various rock bands in the UK, US and Holland.

Paul began writing songs in the late 70s, poetry in the early 90s and eventually his first novel, the children's fantasy, *The Magic Scales*, the first in a series featuring James Peck, in 2008. The books, including the three part *Peck Chronicles,* receiving enthusiastic praise from the charity Asthma UK Scotland for raising awareness of asthma in an engaging fashion.

But it is not just strong young heroes and heroines that Paul writes about. With his regular illustrator, Scott Wallace, he has authored a series of books with animal and numeracy themes, aimed at 3 to 7 year olds – the *Tiffy and Toffy* picture books. This series has been used by UNICEF and other global charities, such as The East Bali Poverty Project, who use the books to teach English and to help younger children with counting.

Passionate about literacy and numeracy, Paul has visited over 200 schools and libraries, engaging over 25,000 children in his performance workshops and presentations designed to fire up young imaginations.

Not content with writing children's and young adult books, Paul also writes gritty thrillers under the name Damian Peck. His first novel as Damian, *The Eden Seed*, was published by Gallus Press in 2014 to great acclaim.

Dividing his time between writing and music, Paul released his solo debut album *Wilderness* in November 2017, which included the single *Golden Rust*, a very personal song written about the effects of living with a loved one suffering from dementia.

Paul can also be spotted onscreen in several TV and film productions including *River City*, *Whisky Galore* and *Tommy's Honour*.

Eunice G Murray MBE

Suffragist, Political Activist & Author
(1878 – 1960)

The Representation of the People Act 1918 gave over eight million women the right to vote. It was followed by the Parliament (Qualification of Women) Act 1918, which enabled women over the age of 21 to stand for election as an MP. Among the first seventeen women ever to stand for parliamentary election – and the first woman to stand for a Scottish seat - was Eunice Guthrie Murray.

Eunice was born on January 21 1878 at Moore Park, Cardross, to David Murray, a Glasgow lawyer, and Frances Porter Stoddard.

Heavily influenced by her parents, Eunice developed a keen interest in civil and human rights and was involved in philanthropic activities from an early age. She was active in the local branch of the children's fundraising organisation the League of Pity and was a keen supporter of the Temperance Movement.

Along with her mother and sister, Eunice joined the Women's Freedom League in 1908 and was soon elected to its National Executive Committee, becoming President of its Scottish council by 1913.

Over the next five years, Eunice balanced suffragist campaigning with support for Britain's war effort, working part time in a munitions factory. Following the passage of the 1918 Acts, she stood for election for the first time as an independent candidate in Glasgow's Bridgeton constituency, coming a distant third.

Despite this setback, Eunice continued to champion women's rights throughout her life, either in person or through her writing, dedicating one book, *Scottish Women of Bygone Days,* to 'The Women of All Ages who Defied Convention and Held Aloft the Banner of Progress.'

In 1923 she was elected to Dunbartonshire county council, and in the same year became the first President of the local Scottish Women's Rural Institute, making significant contributions to both organisations. A founder member of the National Trust for Scotland, Eunice served on its Council and Executive from 1931. In 1945 she was awarded an MBE for her commitment to public service.

Eunice, who never married, died from a stroke on 26 March 1960 at Moore Park in Cardross, which had been her home for eighty two years.

Mary O'Rourke

Singer
(1913 – 1964)

A Helensburgh born woman with a beautiful voice was to become a major recording star performing as a male soprano.

Mary was born to Hannah and Joseph O'Rourke at 6 Maitland Street in Helensburgh on July 26 1913, the twelfth of fourteen children.

With her unique singing voice, Mary won several talent contests during her childhood. After making a name for herself in Scotland's music halls, she moved to London at the age of 17 to further her career. It was here that her entertainer and impresario uncle, Ted Stebbings, taught her to impersonate a boy singer in order to replace one whose voice had recently broken. Mary could imitate a choirboy voice to perfection and so began performing as a boy. At just five feet tall with jet-black hair, she dressed in short trousers and black jacket, her chest bound with bandages.

Appearing as Master Joe Petersen, Mary's popularity with theatre audiences soon led to radio appearances and a recording contract. In 1933, Crystalate Records of London signed her up, billing her as "Master Joe Peterson, the Phenomenal Boy Singer". She became a huge variety star, both in Britain and in Europe.

But Mary was not happy; she did not want what she called the 'boy charade' to continue and wanted to record in her own name. Having become pregnant, she married orchestral violinist George Lethbridge in May1933, but the marriage was an unhappy one. At the outbreak of WW2 George joined the army, leaving Mary to look after their 6-year-old daughter Margot.

The final Master Joe recording was released in 1942.

Mary began to drink heavily. George stayed in the army after the war and their marriage finally collapsed in 1952. Mary returned to live alone in Glasgow, leaving her daughter behind. She continued to perform as Master Joe throughout the 1940s and 1950s, even appearing on STV's One O'clock Show in 1963, at the age of 50.

Mary, by then a chronic alcoholic, died of bronchitis aged 51 at her home on Christmas Eve 1964. She is buried alongside her father, brother Joe and sister Sara in St Peter's Cemetery, Dalbeth, where the inscription reads "Mary Lethbridge, known to her millions of fans as Master Joe Petersen."

Harry Papadopoulos

Photographer

A self-taught photographer from Garelochhead who left teaching to capture the post-punk era as the Indie pop sound of Scotland began to dominate the airwaves.

Harry Papadopoulos was born in Garelochhead in 1954, the son of a Scots mother and Greek-Cypriot father.

Following his school days, Harry graduated from Paisley College of Technology with a degree in electrical engineering before becoming a teacher of maths and physics.

He began his photography career by selling, for fifty pence each, freshly developed black and white prints to concertgoers standing outside the Glasgow Apollo, taken at the artist's Edinburgh gig the previous night.

The quality and style of his pictures began to gain an audience, and Harry headed to London, where he soon came to the attention of the mainstream music press.

Between 1979 and 1984, Harry worked for *New Musical Express* and *Sounds* at the very peak of the new wave music explosion. During this time his photographs covered virtually every major band of the period, including Blondie, David Bowie, Devo, Joy Division and The Clash, with many of his pictures becoming iconic cover images.

Harry also personally captured the rise of Scotland's young and influential artists such as Orange Juice, The Bluebells, Aztec Camera, Altered Images and The Associates, with his North West London flat doubling as a social hub and crash pad for many Scottish bands whenever they found themselves performing in the capital.

Following his stint with the music press, Harry became editor of Marvel Comics before moving into web design.

In August 2002 he suffered a ruptured brain aneurysm and returned to Glasgow. His story might have remained untold had it not been for a chance reconnection – after 20 years - with Ken McCluskey of The Bluebells.

A visit to Harry's flat led Ken to discover more than 3,000 neglected and forgotten negatives capturing the musical and cultural icons of the early 80s.

After eight months of painstaking effort, Ken, working with Harry as part of his long-term rehabilitation, and with Malcolm Dickson of Glasgow's Street Level Photoworks, curated the highly acclaimed touring photographic exhibition and book *What Presence!*

Stephen Park OBE

Sports Performance Director

Even though his parents lived in Helensburgh, Stephen Park - known throughout the sporting community as 'Sparky' - was born in Glasgow on February 24 1968. He attended Hermitage Primary School and Hermitage Academy, and learned his sailing in Mirror dinghies and 420s at Helensburgh Sailing Club.

On leaving Hermitage Academy, he took a BA degree in sport at the Scottish School of Physical Education at Jordanhill, then left home to do an MSc in Recreation Management at Loughborough University followed by a postgraduate diploma in management studies at Newcastle Business School.

After completing his education Stephen went on to work for both the Royal Yachting Association Scotland and the Welsh Yachting Association.

A naturally gifted and talented sailor, he competed in both the 470 and Tornado disciplines at the 1992 and 1996 Olympic Games.

In 2001 the Royal Yachting Association confirmed his appointment as their new Olympic Manager. Athens 2004 was his first Olympics at the helm, and saw Great Britain win five medals in total - two gold, one silver and two bronze – becoming the Games' most successful sailing nation.

At the Beijing games in 2008 expectations were high, and the sailing team did not disappoint. Under Stephen's guidance, the team took medals in six of the eleven contests entered – four golds, a silver and a bronze in events where only one competitor from each country can take part.

Stephen was awarded an OBE in the 2008 New Year's honours list as well as the 2008 Coach of the Year Award at the Sunday Mail and Sport Scotland Scottish Sports Awards.

Sailing hit its medal target of five at London 2012, with the coveted gold for Sir Ben Ainslie and four silver, one of which was won by Helensburgh's Luke Patience.

Stephen continued the success at the 2016 Rio Games with Team GB once again topping the Sailing Medal Table.

In 2017, Stephen swapped Olympic Sports to become British Cycling's first Performance Director since 2014.

He still enjoys sailing, particularly Keelboat racing, has a passion for motorcars and is a keen Formula One fan.

Derek Parlane

Footballer

At the presentation, Derek said: "My father Jimmy played for Rangers in the 1940s and he died a few years ago. This would have been a big night for him and he'd have been so proud of me too … I had 10 great years at Ibrox. I was a supporter first and foremost and this just caps it all perfectly".

Derek James Parlane was born on May 5 1953 in Helensburgh.

He began his football career as a schoolboy playing for Rhu Primary School and then Hermitage Academy. It was whilst playing for the Queen's Park second XI that he got his break. At the age of 15 he was selected to play for Scotland Amateurs in the home Internationals, where he attracted the attention of several clubs.

At age 16, Derek was signed by Willie Waddell and Willie Thornton for Glasgow Rangers. In his time at the club, his team won 2 championships, 3 Scottish Cups and 2 Scottish League Cups; he was capped by Scotland 12 times with one under 21 cap. He played for 10 seasons between 1970 and 1980, scoring 80 goals and finishing four seasons as the club's top scorer.

In March 1980, Derek left Rangers for Leeds United for a fee of £160,000 but it wasn't to prove a successful move. He scored 10 goals in 53 appearances for Leeds before going to Hong Kong on loan with Bulova.

On 14 July 1983 newly appointed manager of Manchester City Billy McNeill brought him to Maine Road, where Derek went on to score 20 goals in 48 appearances for City.

Derek was injured in September 1984 and was sold to Swansea City in January 1985. He then played in New Zealand and Belgium before returning to Britain for two seasons with Rochdale between 1986 and 1988, playing 42 games and scoring 10 times.

His last professional stint was with Airdrie in the 1987–88 season, where he scored 4 goals in 9 games.

Alexander Nisbet Paterson
ARSA FRIBA RSW

Architect
(1862 – 1947)

Born into a family of artists, this talented watercolourist turned architect would help shape the townscape of Helensburgh.

Alexander Nisbet Paterson was born at Berkeley Terrace, Glasgow on May 3 1862, to parents Andrew and Margaret.

Having graduated from Glasgow University with an arts degree in 1882, Alexander wanted to become an artist like his eldest brother James. His parents however could not afford to support two painters in the family, and architecture was decided upon as a compromise. Alexander travelled to Paris and enrolled trat the Ecole des Beaux-Arts in 1883.

In 1886 he returned to Britain to work with James Burnet as an improver and draughtsman, Alexander's artistic skills being much in demand for the presentation of the firm's projects.

In 1889 Alexander passed the Royal Institute of British Architects qualifying exam and won the institute's silver medal before being made an associate on March 3 1890. He then joined the practice of Sir Aston Webb & E Ingress Bell as Webb's assistant before commencing independent practice in Glasgow in 1891.

In 1896 having won a Godwin scholarship, Alexander took a break to visit the USA to study domestic architecture. On his return in 1897 he married Margaret Hamilton, sister of the Glasgow School painter James Whitelaw Hamilton. The couple moved into Turret, one of four houses in Helensburgh his father had financed to help kick start his son's practice.

In 1900, Alexander began planning his private Long Croft home in Rossdhu Drive in Helensburgh, creating a studio within the house to help cope with a burgeoning list of projects, which included the design of the town's Clyde Street School.

Alexander was made associate of the Royal Scottish Academy in 1911 and became a Governor of the Glasgow School of Art in 1916.

Following an operation for throat cancer in 1936 Alexander handed his practice over to John Watson Junior of Watson & Salmond and devoted the rest of his life to watercolour painting.

He died at Long Croft on July 10 1947, and was buried in Helensburgh Cemetery; his family grave is marked by a large Celtic cross designed by fellow architect William Leiper.

Viola Paterson

Artist
(1899 – 1981)

Accomplished Painter, draughtswoman, printmaker and member of the distinguished Paterson family of artists, Mary Viola was born at The Turret, Millig Street, Helensburgh February 19 1899, daughter of Glasgow Architect Alexander Nisbet Patterson and artist Margaret Hamilton. Viola's uncle James was a celebrated member of the Glasgow Boys.

Viola was one of two children – her brother Alastair eschewed the art world in favour of the army and eventually rose to the rank of Major General.

In 1916 Viola began to attend the Slade in London – under Henry Tonks – whilst completing finishing school. She then studied at the Glasgow School of Art under Royal Academician Maurice Greiffenhagen before leaving Scotland in 1924 to study in Paris at L'Academie de la Grande Chaumiere with Lucien Simon Besnard and Andre L'Hote.

Viola continued to paint in France and travelled around Europe before returning to Britain in 1941. During the war she worked for several years for the Admiralty in Oxford. After the war years, Viola settled in Chelsea where she continued to paint and exhibit.

A very capable artist, proficient in all mediums, Viola was renowned for her colour woodcuts which she produced using a technique which she called *Woodtype*. A line drawing would be etched into a soft wood block, creating sections which would be individually coloured with watercolour paints and printed off onto paper, resulting in a complex multi–colour image.

She exhibited widely at The Royal Academy, The Royal Scottish Academy, Royal Glasgow Institute of Fine Arts, The Society of Scottish Artists, and the Belgrave, Parkin and Lillie Galleries.

Viola also designed three stained glass windows for Helensburgh's St Bride's Church, which formerly occupied the site of the current library. The church was demolished in 1990 but the windows were preserved.

Viola returned to her family home, Long Croft, in Helensburgh in 1955. The house was designed by her father to accommodate his own artistic efforts, as well as those of his wife and their circle of artistic friends. Viola described the house as 'embodying much of the last 100 years of Scottish Art'.

Viola lived at Long Croft until her death in 1981.

Luke Patience

Yachtsman

Watching a fellow Scot winning a sailing gold medal at the 2000 Sydney Olympic Games, convinced a fourteen year old Hermitage Academy pupil that anything was possible and that one day he too would find himself on the Olympic podium. He was right.

Luke John Patience was born in Aberdeen on the August 4 1986 but grew up in Rhu, where his father encouraged him to sail from the age of seven. Just two years later Luke was competing in an Optimist in the Scottish Traveller Series.

A pupil at Helensburgh's Hermitage Academy, Luke's heart lay in sport, with Shirley Robertson's Sydney success fuelling his drive and determination to succeed.

Luke entered the British Squad systems and by the age of eighteen had competed at international level in Optimist, 29er and 420 classes, winning several national titles, before moving to the 470 class in preparation for his Olympic dream.

His first years of Olympic campaigning provided a steep learning curve, with regular chopping and changing of sailing partners. Just two weeks before the start of the 2009 World Championships, Luke partnered Stuart Bithell for the first time, the pair returning with the silver medal. Luke and Stuart formed a formidable partnership, winning five medals at European and World Cup Regattas. Their 2011 World Championships silver medal brought Luke the news he had worked so hard for – he was the first Scot to be selected for Team GB's London 2012 Olympic squad.

On August 2 2012, the pair began the first of their 10 races in the 470 class, a series which resulted in an Olympic silver medal.

After London, Luke and Stuart chose to go their separate ways, Luke enjoying continued success with new partners Joe Glanfield and Elliot Willis.

The road to the 2016 Rio Olympics proved a difficult one for Luke. In 2015, he and Elliot were among the first athletes selected for Team GB, but Luke was forced to requalify after Elliot was diagnosed with cancer. Luke teamed up with Chris Grube and the pair won selection, securing a highly commendable fifth place at the Games.

David Peat

Film Maker & Photographer
(1947-2012)

A passion for humanity and the human spirit, led to an award winning forty year career for a man whose lens documented the lives of ordinary people.

David Henderson Peat was born on March 22 1947. On leaving school David worked in a shipping agency but harboured ambitions to become a cameraman. His fascination with photography had begun when his maternal grandmother introduced him to the wonders of the dark room and nurtured his love of black and white photographs. His portfolio of Glasgow photographs in 1968 helped him to enter the relatively new industry of television.

In 1969, David landed a job as an apprentice camera operator; his big break came when he teamed up with the director Murray Grigor to make a series of travelogues, starting with *Travelpass – It's Just the Ticket* in 1972. Their sixth film together was *Clydescope* in 1974, which was presented by shipyard worker-turned-comedian Billy Connolly.

In 1975, David and Murray spent 48 hours following and filming Connolly on a tour across the Ulster/Eire divide at the height of The Troubles in the Seventies. The result was 1976's *Big Banana Feet*.

In the 80's, having worked on a large number of productions, David turned to shooting and directing his own observational films, becoming one of Scotland's leading documentary film makers. Known for his compassion and sense of humour, he was also an inspirational teacher.

Films such as *This Mine is Ours, Gutted, Please Leave the Light On, Big Noise,* to name but a few, won him national and international acclaim.

David received more than twenty major industry awards during his career, his final award being the much coveted BAFTA Scotland Craft Prize for his contribution to the industry.

Throughout his career David was never without his stills camera and the photographs he captured - many housed in the Scottish National Portrait Gallery - along with his documentaries, are now a wonderful legacy.

"It's just that wonderful moment of seeing things – yes – got it – magic"

David, who had lived in Shandon for 27 years, died on April 16 2012 at the age of 65.

Gordon Reid MBE

Wheelchair Tennis Player

Inaugural Wimbledon Men's Wheelchair Singles Champion, four Grand Slam Titles, Gold and Silver Paralympic Medals, World Number One, Freedom of Argyll & Bute – 2016 was the *Year of Gordon Reid*.

Gordon Reid was born on October 2 1991 and grew up in Helensburgh.

At the age of 12, he lived for sport – especially football and tennis, which he began playing at the age of six. However, just a week before his 13th birthday, Gordon started to complain of cramps in his legs. 24 hours later, he was paralysed from the waist down after developing a rare spinal condition, transverse myelitis, and he feared he might never walk again.

Just six months after he was first rushed to hospital, Gordon had won his first wheelchair tennis tournament.

Less than two years later Gordon had risen to the top 100 in the Men's Singles world rankings. At 15 he was Britain's youngest-ever national Men's singles champion and the International Wheelchair Tennis Junior Masters boys' singles champion - all whilst pursuing his studies at Hermitage Academy.

Having reached the Men's top 100, Gordon's aim was to represent Team GB at the Olympics. At the 2008 Beijing games he became the youngest men's tennis player selected to represent Great Britain at a Paralympic Games.

In June 2012, Gordon, ranked as the British Number 1, was selected to represent Team GB again in the London 2012 Paralympics, reaching the quarter-finals of both the Men's Singles and Doubles competitions.

In 2015, Gordon secured his first Grand Slam Titles, winning both the French & US Open Doubles titles.

2016 was a year of remarkable achievement. Gordon won his first Grand Slam Singles title, the Australian Open, the Wimbledon Men's Wheelchair Singles title, the French Wheelchair Doubles title, the Wimbledon Wheelchair Doubles Titles with partner Alfie Hewett and gold and silver medals at the Rio Paralympic Games. He finished the year as the World's Number 1 ranked male wheelchair tennis player.

The year was capped off with Gordon becoming only the second person to be given the freedom of Argyll & Bute and by being awarded the MBE in the New Year's Honours List.

Emma Richards MBE

Yachtswoman

The Around Alone is the longest race for any individual, in any sport, covering some 28,755 miles of the world's roughest and most inhospitable oceans, and it was conquered by a 27 year old from Helensburgh.

Emma Richards was born on October 10 1974. She moved with her parents, Margaret and Bryan, to Scotland in 1980 after her father was appointed to the Chair of Aeronautics and Fluid Mechanics at the University of Glasgow. The family settled in Helensburgh, where Emma attended Lomond School and joined the town's sailing club. By the age of 11 she was competing in world championship dinghy events.

She continued sailing whilst at Glasgow University, and by the time she graduated in 1996 with a BSc in Sports Medicine she was a member of the Scottish National Olympic Training Squad.

At the age of 23, Emma was chosen to join Tracy Edward's all-girl crew aboard Royal Sun Alliance in the Jules Verne Trophy. The yacht was on schedule to set a race record when it lost a mast in the Southern Ocean.

In 2002, Emma became the first British woman and the youngest competitor to complete the Around Alone race. The race, which starts and ends in the US, is staged over five legs.

Emma had only decided to enter the race six weeks before it started, stating: "I have no doubt that this will be the challenge of my life. As well as facing some great competitors and top class boats, the race is going to be both physically and mentally demanding."

And so it proved. Emma spent 132 days at sea alone, the "soul-destroying solitude" as she termed it, aboard a yacht facing hurricane force winds and fending off the unwelcome attention of pirates. She published her own account of her solo voyage, *Around Alone*, in 2004.

In 2003, Emma's remarkable feat was recognised by the award of an MBE in the New Year's Honours List and the title Young Alumnus of the Year by Glasgow University

Emma married New Zealand yachtsman Mike 'Moose' Sanderson on the Isle of Wight in May 2006.

George Rickey

Kinetic Artist
(1907 – 2002)

In the grounds of Helensburgh's iconic Hill House can be found a sinuously moving sculpture 'where the winds of the Clyde estuary keep it in perpetual motion', a gift to the town from one of the world's greatest kinetic artists.

George Rickey was born on June 6 1907 in South Bend, Indiana. In 1913 his father, an executive with Singer Sewing Machine Company, moved the family to Helensburgh.

He grew up in the town, playing with his neighbours' children in the Hill House and sailing on his father's yacht, which was clearly a formative experience; during a 1982 retrospective exhibition of his work in Glasgow, he recalled "I experienced the action of the wind and the laws of motion first hand."

George was educated at Glenalmond College and received a degree in History from Balliol College, Oxford. He spent a short time travelling in Europe and studied art in Paris before returning to the US to begin teaching at the Groton School.

From the early 1950s, George shifted his artistic focus from painting and began creating kinetic sculpture, which combined his love of engineering and mechanics. He was able to design sculptures whose metal parts moved in response to the slightest air currents. These parts were often very large, sometimes weighing several tons.

Most of his work was created in his studio in East Chatham in New York, where he moved after taking a position as Professor of Architecture at Rensselaer Polytechnic Institute. He retired from teaching in 1966 after five years, but continued to make sculpture, keeping studios in Berlin and Santa Barbara. George's last sculpture was also his tallest, measuring 57 feet 1 inch. It was installed at Japan's Hyogo Museum in 2002.

Sadly, Glasgow, a city he loved was to spurn his gift. To celebrate his 1982 retrospective there, George presented the city with a significant piece of sculpture. On the day that it was erected, it was deemed unsafe by a city official, who had it removed to the city's Parks Department outdoor stores from where it was eventually stolen. Helensburgh was more fortunate.

George died in his home in Saint Paul, Minnesota on July 17 2002 at the age of 95.

Rev Archibald Eneas Robertson

Minister & Mountaineer
(1870 – 1958)

Archibald Eneas Robertson is widely credited with being the World's first Munro Bagger.

A Munro is a Scottish mountain with a height of over 3,000 feet, named after Sir Hugh Munro, who compiled a catalogue of such hills, published in the Scottish Mountaineering Club Journal in 1891.

Archie was born in Helensburgh on July 3 1870, where the family lived at a house in what is now Granville Street.

He was educated at a boarding school in Charlotte Street in the town and at Glasgow Academy before graduating from Glasgow University with an MA in Natural Philosophy. In 1892 Archie moved to Edinburgh to study divinity at the city's New College, graduating four years later.

Archie bagged his first Munro – Ben Cruachan – in 1889, and by the time he joined the Scottish Mountaineering Club in 1893 he had amassed a total of 45. Over the next few years he accumulated further peaks at a more modest rate.

During the spring and early summer of 1898 and 1899, he embarked on two major tours, during which he bagged 147 new Munros. He mostly climbed alone, but occasionally with companions including his cousin Kate McFarlan who he married in 1900. The following year, Kate and Archie's friend Sandy Moncrieff was with him when he bagged his final Munro, Meall Dearg.

Although Archie achieved his goal without the aid of motor transport, he made extensive use of the developing rail system and many other forms of transport, in particular the bicycle. He was never without a roof over his head at the end of a day in the hills, and in an era when the glens were more populated, would often overnight at gamekeeper's or shepherd's cottages during his longer treks.

He developed a keen interest in photography after completing the Munros. He was President of the Scottish Mountaineering Club between 1930 and 1932, later becoming an Honorary Member; for a time he was also Chairman of the Scottish Rights of Way Society.

Archie died at his home in Edinburgh on June 22 1858, eleven days shy of his 88th birthday.

Olly Ross

Motorsportsman

Oliphant Biggar Ross was born in Onich, near Fort William, on the December 31 1944.

At the age of nine, he moved with his family to Helensburgh, a town that was not unfamiliar to him having visited it many times to see his Grandparents, who were well known within the Helensburgh community as both sets managed successful businesses in the town. Olly's parents settled in Helensburgh and started the Lennox School of Motoring.

Having completed his education at both Hermitage Primary and Secondary schools, Olly set out on a journey that was to define his next 50 years, and fire his passion for motor cars, when he took over the running of Lennox Car Services garage in Cardross. In 1968 Olly acquired the Kenway School of Motoring and taught generations of local people to drive.

Olly's career as one of Scotland's motor racing greats began in 1964, when, as a young man he began competing in Speed Hill Climb and Sprint events before moving on to circuit racing.

Over the years Olly has competed in more than 30 different cars, from F2 Brabhams, Porsches and Lotuses through to TVRs. Since winning his first title in 1965, he has become a regular sight on the podium, winning an incredible 200 races and over 20 major titles.

Affectionately known as the fastest OAP in Scotland, Olly has raced a Lotus Europa in the Scottish Classic racing series, which he won outright in the 2007 and 2008 seasons, and in which he won the 2 Litre class in 2009.

In 2017 Olly secured a win, a 2nd and a 3rd place at Barbagallo raceway in Wanaroo, Western Australia driving a Chevron B19 sports racing car.

A modest man, Olly attributes his success to two main factors: the ingenuity and expertise of his friends and sponsors and his ability to be both fast and consistent.

He recently stated: "I have been a driving instructor all my life and a qualified motor racing instructor for the past thirty years. The two disciplines are entirely opposite and that's what keeps life interesting."

Dr Kenneth Manley Smith CBE

Virologist & Author
(1892 – 1981)

Kenneth Manley Smith was born in Helensburgh on November 13 1892. He was educated at Dulwich College and at London's Royal College of Science – now Imperial College - where he took his first degree and did graduate research.

After having graduated with second-class honours in 1914 he almost immediately enlisted as a private in the 14th Battalion of the London Scottish Regiment. He was invalided out of the service in 1915.

Kenneth worked as a lecturer in Agricultural Entomology at Manchester University between 1920 and 1927 before moving to Cambridge to work at the newly-created Potato Virus Station, where he was appointed Director in 1939. During his tenure as Director, he had an immense influence in the establishment of virology, both through his writing and through pioneering research into both plant and insect viruses. Although he was perhaps less analytical than most modern scientists, he unravelled many intricate biological problems with the limited resources at his disposal.

His books on virology have become the standard texts for many an aspiring student and he was absolutely committed to making the subject of virology as accessible and popular as possible.

He remained Director of the Potato Virus Station until his retirement in 1959 when, after various changes, it was renamed the Virus Research Unit.

He was made a CBE in 1956.

In retirement he continued active research in the USA between 1962 and 1969, after which he returned to Cambridge to concentrate on new and revised publications.

A keen cyclist, Kenneth disliked cars and insisted on cycling the 5 miles to and from the Virus Station throughout his working life. In retirement – and after two hip replacements - he installed an exercise bicycle in his home that he used each day.

Kenneth was described in an obituary as being "A reserved man with firm opinions that he never forced on people … Always the perfect gentleman, he never raised his voice in argument but his masterly command of English and his keen dry wit were powerful weapons which added interest and dimension to any subject".

Kenneth died on the June 11 1981.

Walter Smith OBE

Footballer & Manager

Walter Smith was born on February 24 1948 in Lanark, grew up in the East End of Glasgow, and has spent many years with his family in Helensburgh.

Walter began his football career in the 1960s with Junior League team Ashfield. He signed as a defender with Dundee United in 1966, joining as a part-timer while still working as an electrician. At the age of 29, a pelvic injury threatened his playing career and he was invited to join the Dundee United coaching staff.

In 1978 he was appointed coach of the Scotland Under 18 team, helping them to win the European Youth Championship in 1982. He then became coach of the Under 21 team, and was Alex Ferguson's assistant manager during the 1986 Mexico World Cup.

In 1986, Walter became assistant manager at Rangers FC. He was instrumental in their success over the following years, taking over the first team as manager in April 1991.

Seven successive league titles followed under Walter's tenure, including a domestic treble in 1992/93. He also won both the Scottish Cup and the League Cup three times each.

In 1997 he led Rangers to their record-equalling ninth successive League title and was awarded the OBE for services to football in the Queen's birthday honours list.

A three-season spell at Everton was to follow before Walter was again called back north of the border in December of 2004 – this time as manager of the national side. He is credited with rejuvenating the Scottish squad. When he left the job, Scotland were Group B leaders in the Euro 2008 qualifying phase, and the team's FIFA world ranking had improved by 70 places.

A return to Rangers in 2007 proved hugely successful, with a UEFA Cup final and the SPL and Scottish Cup double. On 25 April 2010, Walter led Rangers to their 53rd title before announcing that the following season would be his last.

His final season resulted in the securing of a domestic double, with Rangers winning the League Cup as well as a 54th league championship, a world record.

Charlotte Cooper Sterry

Tennis Player
(1870 – 1966)

The distinction of being the first woman ever to become an Olympic Champion goes to an extraordinary sportswoman who won the tennis singles title at the 1900 Paris Games and spent the later years of her life in Helensburgh.

Charlotte Reinagle Cooper was born in Ealing, Middlesex, on September 22 1870, to Henry Cooper, a miller, and his American-born wife Teresa.

Nicknamed Chattie, Charlotte was a tall, slender, elegant but deceptively powerful athlete. She learned her sport at Ealing Lawn Tennis Club, where she won her first tournament aged 14.

After winning her first senior singles title in 1893, Charlotte - the first female tennis player to serve overhead – went on to win five Ladies Singles Wimbledon Championships, reaching 11 finals in total. Her attacking style game won her many admirers and she quickly became a role model for young women in sport.

Charlotte's first Wimbledon title was won in 1895 and her last in 1908, when at 37 years and 296 days she became, and still remains, Wimbledon's oldest Ladies' Singles Champion. In addition she won many doubles and mixed doubles titles throughout her career. What is even more remarkable about Charlotte's sporting achievements is that she won most of her titles whilst completely deaf, having lost her hearing at the age of 26.

In 1900, at the Summer Olympic Games in Paris, Charlotte became the first woman to win an Olympic gold medal by taking the Women's Singles title, also winning the mixed doubles title at the games.

On January 12 1901, Charlotte married Alfred Sterry, a solicitor, and continued playing under her married name. The couple had two children, Rex and Gwen, Charlotte becoming only the second of four women to win the Wimbledon Ladies' Singles after becoming a mother.

In 1912, at the age of 41, she made it to her last Wimbledon finals.

Charlotte continued to play tennis throughout her seventies, moving to Helensburgh after Alfred died to be near her daughter.

Charlotte spent the last years of her life in the town. She passed away aged 96 at 19 Cumberland Avenue, Helensburgh on October 10 1966.

Richard Tait

Entrepreneur

This is the simple mantra by which one man has lived his life, a man who has always believed in the incredible personal empowerment that dreaming brings. The freedom to dream, in his mind being the greatest gift bestowed upon him by his parents Tom and Kathleen.

Born in Broughty Ferry near Dundee in 1965, Richard Tait spent his formative years in Helensburgh, attending both Hermitage Primary School and Hermitage Academy, where he developed a keen interest in computing.

Having graduated from Edinburgh's Heriot-Watt University with an honours degree in computer science, and finding opportunities limited in the UK, Richard headed to the US, completing an MBA at Dartmouth College, New Hampshire.

In 1988, Richard joined Microsoft, where he launched more than a dozen start-ups. He helped pioneer client server computing and built the company's CD ROM business by developing the multi-media encyclopaedia Encarta, and became 1994's Employee of the Year.

In 1997, Richard left Microsoft, and along with fellow executive Whit Alexander founded Cranium Inc. which quickly became the World's third-largest games company, selling more than 40 million board games in 22 countries with Cranium winning the Toy Industry Association's Game of the Year five years in a row.

In creating Cranium, Richard also challenged established retail practise by taking the game directly to its target customers rather than wait for them to find it on the shelves of toyshops.

After Cranium was sold to Hasbro in January 2008 for approximately $77m, Richard started an innovation lab in Seattle – BoomBoom brands – rolling out a number of start-up companies.

In April 2016, Richard was appointed senior vice president and entrepreneur in residence for Starbucks to assist the company in fostering a culture of innovation.

Richard is a member of the Collegiate Entrepreneurs Organization Hall of Fame in the United States and the Entrepreneurial Exchange Hall of Fame in Scotland.

In 2013 he was presented with the honorary degree of Doctor of Letters from Heriot-Watt University for his outstanding and innovative contribution to the advancement of business leadership and entrepreneurship.

Major-General Philip Thomas Tower
CB DSO MBE

Army Officer
(1917 – 2006)

Philip Thomas Tower was born in Rhu on March 1 1917, the only son of Vice-Admiral Sir Thomas Tower. He was educated at Harrow and at the Royal Military Academy in Woolwich, before being commissioned into the Royal Artillery in 1937 where he served with 25 Field Regiment RA in India until the outbreak of World War II.

Ordered to North Africa, Philip saw active service against the Italians in 1940 and 1941 and was at the Battle of Bir Hakeim in May 1942, after which he was awarded an MBE.

In June 1942, at Tobruk, his battery was surrounded after its ammunition was exhausted and he was forced to surrender. He was awarded the Distinguished Service Order for his part in this action.

Philip was taken prisoner and interned in a POW camp in Italy until the Italian armistice was signed in September 1943, after which he escaped, travelled south through the mountains for two months and was wounded in the chest by a mine before he finally reached the Allied lines.

Philip was appointed Brigade Major of the 1st Airborne Division in April 1944. At Arnhem, he parachuted in, and although he was later safely evacuated, the desperate battle remained one of his most poignant memories. The following year, he accompanied 1st Air Landing Regiment in the relief of Norway.

After the war Philip attended Staff College and joined the Royal Military Academy Sandhurst as an instructor.

In 1967, he was appointed a Companion of the Order of the Bath and became Commandant at Sandhurst. In May of the same year, he became General Officer Commanding Middle East Land Forces and served in the Aden Emergency.

On his return to the UK in 1967 he was appointed CB and became Commander of RMA Sandhurst, a post he held until his retirement from the Army in 1972.

Following his military career, Philip was administrator of the National Trust property Blickling Hall in Norfolk between 1973 and 1982 and served as County Commissioner for the Norfolk St John Ambulance Brigade between 1975 and 1978.

He died on December 8 2006, aged 89.

Captain Ernest J D Turner
CBE DSO DSC DL Croix de Guerre

Royal Navy Officer
(1914 – 2007)

Ernest John Donaldson Turner was born in Helensburgh on March 21 1914 to parents Ernest and Margaret. Turner's father was tragically lost at sea with Lord Kitchener and 744 others in the sinking of HMS Hampshire in 1916, when Ernest was just two.

Educated at Hermitage Academy in Helensburgh and at Glasgow Technical College, Ernest joined the Merchant Navy with the Glasgow-based Henderson Line in March 1930. He then joined the Royal Naval Reserve before transferring to the Royal Navy in 1938. He served on both HMS Resolution and HMS Hussar before volunteering for the submarine service in 1939.

In 1940 he became liaison officer of the French submarine Rubis. Operating in Norwegian waters out of a base in Dundee, the Rubis sank five enemy ships in six weeks; two of them on the same day. Ernest was awarded the Distinguished Service Cross in January 1941, also receiving the Croix de Guerre from the French authorities.

Throughout 1941, he served as First Lieutenant on the Gibraltar-based submarine HMS Clyde, sinking enemy shipping and patrolling from the Mediterranean to the South Atlantic.

In 1942, Ernest completed the gruelling submarine commanding officer's qualifying course. At the age of 28, he was appointed to command HMS Sibyl which went on to sink several enemy ships during her 17 patrols in the Mediterranean. Ernest was subsequently awarded the Distinguished Service Order for his actions.

Ernest stayed on in the Navy after the war and held many senior appointments both in the UK and overseas. In 1965 he became Captain-in-Charge Clyde and was heavily involved in preparations for the arrival of the Polaris nuclear system at Faslane. He eventually became Commander of the base before retiring from the Navy in 1968. On relinquishing command, he was appointed CBE in the Queen's Birthday Honours list in June 1968.

He then worked for Clyde Port Authority before re-joining the MoD as Senior Schools Liaison Officer, responsible for Royal Navy and Royal Marines recruitment in Scotland and Northern England.

Ernest died at the age of 92 on March 2 2007, and was buried with full Royal Naval honours.

Mary Ure

Actress
(1933 – 1975)

Eileen Mary Ure was born on February 18 1933 in Glasgow to parents Colin and Edith.

Mary's grandfather was the prosperous flour merchant John Ure, who lived in the magnificent Leiper-designed Cairndhu House in Helensburgh.

Mary spent her early years at her home with her parents in Kilcreggan before being sent away to a Quaker boarding school in York.

After a nationwide search she was chosen to play the Virgin Mary in a revival of the York Mystery Plays in 1951. The play's producers sent Mary to study at the Central School of Speech Training and Dramatic Art in London. In 1954 she made her professional stage debut in Manchester.

Her first film appearance was in *Storm Over the Nile* in 1955. The following year she played the role of Alison Porter in John Osborne's *Look Back in Anger* at the Royal Court theatre in London. She married Osborne in 1957, but within a year the marriage was in trouble. Osborne's infidelities and abusive behaviour saw Mary become more and more dependant on alcohol.

Mary reprised her role as Alison in the 1959 film adaptation of *Look Back in Anger*, which also starred Richard Burton. Her portrayal of Clara Dawes in 1960's *Sons and Lovers* earned Mary an Academy Award nomination.

In 1963, following her divorce from Osborne, she married Robert Shaw and returned to cinema in *The Mind Benders*. Further film roles were to follow, most notably in 1968's *Where Eagles Dare* alongside Richard Burton and Clint Eastwood. However, Robert Shaw was fiercely protective – and perhaps jealous - of his wife, and persuaded her to step back from acting to concentrate on motherhood.

Mary's final film was to be 1972's *A Reflection of Fear* alongside Shaw, but by then her problems with alcohol were getting worse. Her return to theatre - in a 1974 Broadway production of Congreve's *Love for Love* - ended suddenly following a disastrous matinee performance.

On April 2 1975 she returned to the London stage in *The Exorcism*, but just a few hours after the play had opened, Mary died of an accidental overdose. She was 42.

Professor George Urquhart FRCVS

Parasitologist
(1925 – 1997)

George MacDonald Urquhart was born in Glasgow on May 29 1925.

On graduating from the Glasgow Veterinary College as the gold medallist in 1947, he was awarded a scholarship to work with Dr E L Taylor in the parasitology department at Weybridge. He returned to Glasgow in 1949 as one of a group charged with taking the old Glasgow College into the university system. George played a leading role in the development and recognition of the college as a veterinary research institution of international standing.

In 1957 George moved to Kenya where he researched a range of parasitic diseases. A notable success came with the development, in collaboration with Bill Jarrett, Ian McIntyre, Bill Mulligan and others, of the Dictol vaccine to combat parasitic bronchitis in cattle.

On his return to Scotland in the early 1960s he and his colleagues carried out in-depth studies of parasitic gastritis in cattle.

In 1964 the Wellcome Trust supported the construction of laboratories at Bearsden, which became the base for George's scientific activities for the next 26 years. In 1979, the first and only Chair of Veterinary Parasitology in the UK was created at Glasgow to which George Urquhart was rightly appointed.

George's love affair with Africa continued beyond his retirement when he agreed to take up an appointment for one year as director general of the International Trypanotolerance Centre in The Gambia, which was at a crucial point in its development.

George was President of the World Association for the Advancement of Veterinary Parasitology from 1985 to 1989 and was elected to the Royal Society of Edinburgh in1990. He was also an honorary fellow of the Royal College of Veterinary Surgeons and an honorary member of the British Society of Parasitology.

Sailing was George's love throughout most of his life. During the 20 years he lived in Helensburgh he was able to enjoy the sailing opportunities that the area provided. The freedom and fresh air of the sea supplied George with the space and time to develop many of his ideas.

Described in an obituary as an 'Intellectual Giant'. George died on January 13 1997.

Tom Vaughan

Film & Television Director

"The Logie Baird TV set in the local library was a constant reminder that you can come from a small town like Helensburgh and go out into the world and do whatever you want."

Tom Vaughan was born in Glasgow on September 5 1969 and spent the first 17 years of his life in Helensburgh. He attended the town's Hermitage Academy, where he was a classmate of acclaimed digital artist Laura Grieve.

Tom cut his creative teeth as a child actor in the TV show *Stookie*, but his true calling lay behind the lens. He used his earnings from Stookie to purchase his own video camera and embarked on his fledgling movie career by making films with his friends all over Helensburgh. He recalls: "We would go behind the house, near the naval base and out on the playing fields and shoot comedies, war movies, anything really."

After Tom left school he graduated in Drama at Bristol University and in 1990 moved to London to concentrate on making short films. His first short *Super Grass* went on to win a distribution deal with Richard Linklater's movie *Dazed and Confused,* playing in cinemas across the country before being bought by Film Four and shown on national TV.

Within a year, Tom had shot several TV commercials and won a BTAA Gold Arrow for his work on a *Yellow Pages* campaign.

Over the next few years, Tom juggled commercial work with TV drama series such as *Cold Feet, I Saw You* and *Final Demand.*

He made his feature film-directing debut with the 2006 coming of age comedy *Starter for Ten* which starred James McAvoy. For his second feature, Tom travelled to the US to direct Cameron Diaz and Ashton Kutcher in the 2008 hit romantic comedy *What Happens in Vegas.*

One of Tom's career highlights was directing Harrison Ford in 2009's *Extraordinary Measures,* having been originally inspired to become a filmmaker by watching *Star Wars* in Helensburgh's La Scala cinema.

In recent years Tom has spent much of his time directing for TV, where his directing credits include *Doctor Foster, Endeavour, The Royals, The Son, Press* and *Victoria,* for which he received a BAFTA Scotland nomination.

Kyle Warren

Musician

"The difference between talent and skill is simple: Talent can help you get to the top, skill is what keeps you there."

Born May 7 1988 and raised in Helensburgh, former Hermitage Academy pupil Kyle Warren began learning the bagpipes at the age of eight, having been inspired by his father, uncle and grandfather.

He excelled at the instrument and soon became an influential member of the Lomond and Clyde Pipe Band. In 2008 Kyle played with the famous Strathclyde Police Pipe Band – Scotland's premier grade one pipe ensemble.

Aged 14, Kyle was among the first intake of pipers for the National Youth Pipe Band of Scotland. During his time with the NYPB, Kyle rose to the position of Pipe Major, performed overseas and appeared on BBC TV's *Blue Peter*.

With the support of the Royal Caledonian Education Trust, Kyle was able to take lessons at the National Piping Centre before starting a piping degree course at the Royal Conservatoire of Scotland in 2006.

In 2007, Kyle formed the world's first bagpipe boy band, TNT – The New Tradition – with two friends, with the aim of making bagpiping 'cool' to attract a new generation of listeners. TNT won the prestigious Danny Kyle Open Stage competition at Celtic Connections in 2007.

Kyle was soon in demand and he started touring extensively with the renowned Red Hot Chilli Pipers in 2009. Following a two year stint on the road, Kyle left the group to concentrate on his own music and his teaching career. It was to herald the start of an extraordinary period of success.

In May 2011, Kyle released his debut album *Wanted*, which included many of his own compositions. One year later and he was to return to the recording studio to perform on the soundtrack of the Oscar-winning Disney Pixar film *Brave*.

By the end of 2013, Kyle had won 13 International titles, including the piping "grand slam" of the Cowal, Scottish, British, European and World Piping Championships as part of the Field Marshall Montgomery pipe band.

Having emigrated in 2014, Kyle lives and teaches music in Melbourne, Australia.

Sir Cecil McAlpine Weir
KCMG KBE MC DL

Industrialist & Civic Administrator
(1890 – 1960)

Cecil McAlpine Weir was born at Bridge of Weir, Renfrewshire, on July 5 1890, the youngest of four sons of Alexander Cunningham Weir and his wife, Isabella McLeish.

He was educated at Morrison's Academy, Crieff, and in Switzerland and Germany. Upon completing his studies, he returned to Scotland and undertook two years in business studies before becoming a partner in his father's leather and hide business in Glasgow.

During the First World War, Cecil served with distinction in both France and at Gallipoli, where he was wounded and earned the Military Cross for his courage.

In 1915 Weir married Jenny Paton, and the couple settled in Helensburgh, purchasing the White House at 15 Colquhoun Street with its magnificent views across the Gare Loch.

Between the wars, Cecil became especially well known for his enthusiasm and active participation as a member of the Glasgow Chamber of Commerce, where he was to eventually hold the office of President between 1939 and 1941.

It was Cecil's imagination and passion for the business and enterprise that led him to formulating the idea for creating and holding an Empire Exhibition in Glasgow, an idea for which he obtained wide support. The 1938 exhibition achieved a large measure of success and Cecil was appointed KBE in recognition of his efforts.

His business acumen and organisational skills brought Cecil to the attention of the War Office, and in August 1939 he was appointed Civil Defence Commissioner for the Western District of Scotland before serving as Director General of Equipment and Stores at the Ministry of Supply.

Upon leaving the Ministry in 1946, Cecil took the post of Economic Advisor to the Allied Control Commissions for Germany followed by two years as Chairman of the Dollar Exports Board.

It was about this time that Cecil sold the White House in Helensburgh and began dividing his time between properties in both Luxembourg and London.

He was appointed KCMG in 1952 and was also, in this same year, elected President of the Institution of Production Engineers.

Cecil died at his home, 19 Thorney Court in Kensington, on October 30 1960.

Kim Winser OBE

Businesswoman

Touted as a potential British tennis star at seventeen, she forsook that path for another: a career in the retail business – a choice that would transform the fortunes of luxury fashion brands Pringle of Scotland, Aquascutum and Agent Provocateur.

Kim Lesley Haresign was born on March 11 1959 in Helensburgh, where her father served in the Navy. The family moved to Portsmouth when Kim was three. From the age of thirteen Kim had worked every weekend in both a shoe shop and a newsagents, fuelling her passion for the retail business.

A straight-A pupil, Kim was a high achiever at school, becoming Head Girl of Purbrook Park Grammar School. However, she chose not to go to university, instead accepting a place on Marks & Spencer's management training scheme at her father's recommendation.

Her 23-year career with M&S was both impressive and groundbreaking, and saw her progressing from trainee to youngest and first female Board member and Director of Womenswear. Under her direction, the business grew substantially in sales, market share and profit and the company scrapped its archaic rules to allow women to join the board via a commercial route.

In 2000, Kim left M&S and was appointed CEO of Pringle, with the task of transforming one of the world's oldest fashion labels from 'frumpy to fabulous'. Within three months of Kim's arrival a new collection was designed and launched, and a powerful brand strategy implemented. In the six years that Kim held the position, flagship stores were opened across the globe, models paraded the clothes on the world's catwalks and turnover rose from £10M to £100M per year.

In 2006 Kim was appointed President and CEO of Aquascutum and, in 2010, Chairman of Agent Provocateur, repositioning both brands into the luxury sector.

Recognising an important gap in the market for a brand offering luxurious quality women's clothes cut to flatter all ages and figures, Kim launched her own company – Winser London – in 2013.

Described by Business Week as 'the most innovative businesswomen in Britain', Kim was awarded an OBE for services to the fashion industry in 2006.

Ryan Young

Musician

His style of fiddle playing has been described as both 'ground breaking' and 'a welcome breath of fresh air', whilst his impact on the traditional music scene has been termed 'an earthquake of a sensation'.

Ryan Young was born on October 27 1990 at the Vale of Leven hospital.

His passion for music, and specifically the fiddle, was inspired by three key events. The first was seeing the Scottish music legend Aly Bain perform on a BBC Hogmanay show, the second was his being selected to play violin by highly-respected music teacher Helen Reid-Foster in his fourth year at Cardross Primary School. The third was experiencing a bewitching fiddle performance by musician Eilidh Steel at a Helensburgh and Lomond Fiddlers Group session.

All three combined to convince Ryan that his future lay with the fiddle.

Throughout his final primary years and early teens at Hermitage Academy, Ryan nurtured his musical development, receiving tuition from inspiring musicians such as Eilidh, Helen Reid-Foster, Kirsty Cotter, James Ross and Sarah-Jane Summers.

Aged just 15, Ryan was awarded the Associated Board of the Royal Schools of Music scholarship to attend the Royal Conservatoire of Scotland Junior Academy. He later entered the Senior Academy, receiving the Arthur Robertson prize for Scots fiddle playing during his third year before graduating with a first-class honours degree in Scottish Music.

Public recognition for his talent has been a constant throughout Ryan's musical career. In 2007 he was a winner of the Danny Kyle Open Stage at Glasgow's Celtic Connections festival, a 2007 and 2008 finalist in the BBC Radio 2 Young Folk Awards, a 2015 and 2016 BBC Radio Scotland Young Traditional Musician of the Year finalist and was named Up and Coming Artist of the Year at the 2016 MG Alba Scots Trad Music Awards.

Influenced by the fiddle playing of County Clare, and giving new life to old and largely forgotten Scottish tunes, his live performances have captivated audiences all over the world.

Ryan released his self-titled debut album, produced by the American triple Grammy award winner Jesse Lewis, to great critical acclaim in August of 2017.

Anna Zinkeisen

Artist
(1901 – 1976)

Having grown up on the Clyde, this Kilcreggan-born artist was destined to return professionally some thirty years later to paint the panel murals on the ballroom aboard the John Brown & Company-built RMS Queen Mary.

Anna Katrina Zinkeisen, younger sister of fellow artist Doris, was born on August 29 1901 at Woodburn in Kilcreggan to parents Victor and Clare.

Anna was educated at home until the family moved to Middlesex in 1909, where she attended the Harrow School of Art. She won a scholarship to the Royal Academy Schools, and studied there between 1917 and 1921, eventually transferring to the Sculpture School at the suggestion of her tutor Sir William Orpen.

Anna's work at the school won both silver and bronze medals, bringing her to the attention of the Wedgewood company. She was commissioned to design bas-relief plaques, becoming the first person since John Flaxman in 1775 to provide original Wedgwood designs.

Although Anna's designs won her a silver medal at the Exposition des Art Decoratifs in Paris in 1925, she decided to specialise in painting.

Anna's work was much in demand. She was regularly commissioned to paint portraits of society figures, produce advertising materials and illustrations for books and magazine covers. In addition to her work aboard RMS Queen Mary in 1935, Anna also worked on the RMS Queen Elizabeth in 1940.

In 1928, Anna married army colonel Guy Heseltine and, shortly before the outbreak of WW2, she had her only child Julia, who would become a renowned artist in her own right.

During World War II, Anna worked as a Medical Artist and nursing auxiliary in the Order of St John at St. Mary's Hospital, Paddington, tending to - and drawing - air-raid victims. During this period Anna would use a disused operating theatre as a studio, and she became highly skilled in anatomical drawing – her work being favourably compared to that of Leonardo Da Vinci.

After the War both sisters relocated from London to Suffolk - Doris to Badingham and Anna to Woodbridge.

Anna would continue painting until she passed away in London on September 23 1976.

Doris Zinkeisen

Artist & Theatrical Designer
(1898 – 1991)

Trained as an artist, Doris Zinkeisen developed her realist style to become one of the greatest stage designers of the inter-war years, befriending many of the leading theatrical personalities of the time.

Doris Clare Zinkeisen was born at Clynder House, Clynder on July 31 1898.

With sister Anna, Doris studied art in Harrow and won a scholarship to the Royal Academy Schools. A prodigious talent, Doris' first portrait, a study of Anna that she painted when she was 16, was exhibited at the Royal Academy in 1918.

During the 1920s and 30s, Doris shared a London studio with Anna with the pair considered the 'bright young things' of the art world. Doris in particular gathered a reputation for society portraiture and for scenes that reflected the lifestyle of the rich and famous.

Early in her career, Doris met Sir Nigel Playfair, actor-manager of the Lyric Theatre, Hammersmith, who introduced her to the impresario Charles B Cochran. This meeting led Doris to take the position of chief stage and costume designer for Cochran's popular London Reviews.

Writing in the Studio Magazine in 1927, Cochran said of Doris: "This young decorator, at her early age is, in my opinion, in the front rank of British designers".

Although Doris considered the theatre her home, she also designed costumes for a dozen films, including 1932's *Good Night Vienna* starring Helensburgh's Jack Buchanan.

In 1948 Doris published her book *Designing for the Stage*, which is considered one of the greatest works on the subject.

Doris joined the St John Ambulance Brigade at the outbreak of World War II, and was later commissioned by the Red Cross and St John War Organisation to travel overseas as a war artist.

In 1945, she entered Bergen-Belsen concentration camp, spending three days capturing the horror that she witnessed. Her most famous work from this period, *Human Laundry*, was described by the Imperial War Museum as 'arguably the most powerful work produced by any of the artists who were present'.

After the war had ended, Doris moved to Suffolk where she continued working until her death on January 3 1991.

HELENSBURGH HER✺ES

Images and Credits

The guiding principle underpinning the foundation of Helensburgh Heroes was that every member of a community has something to offer and contribute and, by doing so, can become a hero, if only for a day.

Our vision is that by celebrating our past we may inspire and shape our future.

HELENSBURGH HER✪ES

For further information about Helensburgh Heroes
www.helensburghheroes.com

Helensburgh Heroes is a Charity registered in Scotland SC040114

Lightning Source UK Ltd.
Milton Keynes UK
UKOW05f2305181117

312915UK00004B/158/P